WILFRID BLUNT'S EGYPTIAN GARDEN

∞⊰⊱∞

uncovered editions

Titles in the series

uncovered editions

WILFRID BLUNT'S EGYPTIAN GARDEN: FOX-HUNTING IN CAIRO

∞⚬⚭⚬∞

London: The Stationery Office

First published 1901 Cd. 796
© Crown Copyright

This abridged edition
© The Stationery Office 1999
Reprinted with permission.

ISBN 0 11 702416 3

A CIP catalogue record for this book is available from the
British Library.

Printed in the UK by Biddles Limited, Guildford, Surrey
J93521   C50   11/99

Uncovered Editions are historic official papers which have not previously been available in a popular form. The series has been created directly from the archive of The Stationery Office in London, and the books have been chosen for the quality of their story telling. Some subjects are familiar, but others are less well known. Each is a moment of history.

At the time of this correspondence Egypt had been in the protection of the British Empire since 1882. In 1901, in order to provide sport for the officers, a pack of hounds was shipped out from England to hunt the Egyptian fox.

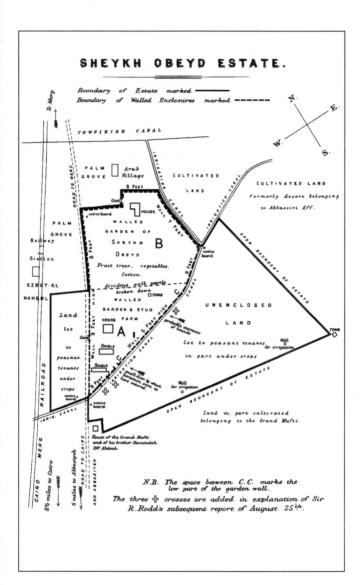

SHEYKH OBEYD ESTATE.

Boundary of Estate marked ———
Boundary of Walled Enclosures marked - - - - -

N.B. The space between C.C. marks the low part of the garden wall.

The three ✠ crosses are added in explanation of Sir R. Rodd's subsequent report of August 25ᵗʰ.

NO. 1.

Sir R. Rodd to the Marquess of Lansdowne.—(Received July 23.)

(Telegraphic)   Cairo, July 23, 1901

ON Sunday morning a fox-hunt was taking place near Cairo, in the desert, the hounds following a scent crossed the boundary-wall of Mr. Wilfrid Blunt's property, and two of the field, being British officers, who were acting as whips, went in to turn them back.

Mr. Blunt's watchmen surrounded them, and, although they explained their intention, treated them with considerable violence. The senior officer present approached, and strictly forbade any attempt at retaliation. The overseer of the property helped in procuring the names of the aggressors. An inquiry is proceeding, and action will be taken against the chief offenders.

The officers were all dressed in mufti, and no special importance attaches itself to the matter, but it is necessary to show clearly that private servants in charge of landed property will not be permitted to use personal violence in order to prevent trespassing.

NO. 2

Mr. Wilfrid Blunt to the Marquess of Lansdowne.—(Received July 27.)

Fernycroft, Beaulieu, Hants, July 25, 1901

My Lord,

I VENTURE to bring before your Lordship's official notice a paragraph published to-day in the "Standard" and other newspapers recording an incident which has just happened on my property in Egypt, and which has been confirmed to me by a private telegram announcing the arrest there of the Arab manager of my stud and two native guards.

Although I have not yet received full particulars, the fact of this arrest obliges me to write at once to your Lordship, before whom the matter will, no doubt, have been brought, asking that you will be good enough, through the Cairo Agency, to make it known to whatever body may be conducting the inquiry that, much as I regret the incident, I accept the full responsibility of my servants' action. As far as I can learn they have simply carried out the general instructions I always give them during my summer absence to allow no one within my walled garden while I am away on any pretence, and least of all of sport. My order to them was very positive, and should be taken into account in any decision come to about them. It is true it did not contemplate an invasion of English fox-hunters, for fox-hunting is a complete novelty of the present summer in that part of Egypt, but being general it necessarily in their minds included it.

Having said thus much in exculpation of my servants, your Lordship will allow me, I hope, to add some words as to the general circumstances of the case which have led to the unfortunate collision. In Egypt, owing to the extreme laxity of the laws protecting native cultivators from injury at the hands of European trespassers, especially in pursuit of game, and the privileged position held by these in the Law Courts, much wrong is every year inflicted on the fellahin, and ill-feeling aroused, for which there is no legal remedy. European sportsmen, who are principally Greeks and Italians in pursuit of small birds, hold by long immunity that it is their right to march through the standing crops of the peasantry, to enter even inclosed grounds, and to discharge their firearms as they please without regarding the damage done or the safety of the cultivators at work in them. Instances constantly occur in a country so highly cultivated and so populous as is the Delta of gun-shot wounds through the carelessness of shooters, and of loss to poor people on highly-taxed land who can afford no loss.

Against this, under existing circumstances, the native proprietor has no remedy. It is practically impossible for him to sue the trespasser for damage in the international Courts, and where bodily hurt has been inflicted he is not allowed personally to arrest the European—his only possible means of identifying him in the general absence of all rural police. Any attempt of the kind would expose him to arrest and detention—it might be for weeks or months—without the smallest chance of redress at the end of it. I have constantly brought the injustice thus suffered before those in power in Cairo, and I have as constantly found my observations received sympathetically.

I believe I am right in saying that both Lord Cromer and Mr. Machell, the English adviser of the Ministry of the Interior, are in favour of strengthening the law of trespass, and I know that excellent regulations have been drafted, though for one reason and another they have remained unpromulgated in the Ministerial port-folios. They are the more required because they are the only practical way of arresting the destruction of bird-life in Egypt—a matter of such great importance to the world at large. The principal obstacle would seem to have been the difficulty of persuading the many European Governments internationally interested in Egypt to surrender any privilege, however unjust, enjoyed against the native Egyptians by their subjects residing there.

Under these circumstances, it seems to me singularly unfortunate that officers of the English garrison at Cairo, at a moment when the native Ministry, guided by our diplomacy, are trying, as I believe they are trying, to introduce a more reasonable law of trespass, should have brought this novelty of fox-hunting into a country wholly unsuited for it. If it were possible to confine the thing to the desert it might be tolerated as harmless, but both foxes and jackals cling to the shelter of the cultivated fields and gardens, and cannot be hunted without interfering with these. Trespass, therefore, is a necessity of the case, and on lands cultivated in small holdings like allotment gardens by very poor people paying immensely high taxes. My own inner walled garden, where the incident occurred, pays as much as 30s. an acre land tax for its 33 acres. I have preserved foxes in it for many years for the inestimable service they render in the destruction of rats, the plague of the Delta, as well as in deference to the ancient toleration public opinion has from all time accorded them in Egypt. To destroy these quite harmless animals for the sake of a little very doubtful sport and to the disturbance and trouble of the whole country round seems to me a very foolish proceeding. As sport it is really unworthy of Englishmen. The Egyptian fox is a small unventuresome beast, too tame and familiar with mankind to be treated as a true wild animal. In my garden they are hardly less tame than the village dogs, and I have known them even outside in the desert refuse to move away from a passing rider. They cannot be made to run after the fashion of English foxes, and it is mere butchery to kill them. For thousands of years they have been treated only with kindness by the fellahin.

With regard to the "assault" on the English officers, I am sorry for it. In the twenty years that I have owned my property in Egypt, though I have had occasional trouble with trespassers of other nationalities, no Englishman has forced his way in that character within my wall, and if I had been there I need not say the hunters would have been received with all possible politeness, but I would suggest to them that, even according to the most liberal interpretation of fox-hunting rights in England, they were in the wrong in not having applied to me, in starting their new pack, for leave to "draw my covers" or to follow their fox through them. I don't say that the leave would have been accorded, for I consider fox-hunting out of place and somewhat childish as a sport in Egypt, but the application would have been more in accordance with hunting etiquette, and, at least, it would have enabled me to give warning to my servants to deal with them becomingly. I had heard no word of the hunt being in existence until yesterday's collision was announced.

I feel sure, my Lord, that this explanation given, you will think it right to communicate its substance without delay to Cairo, where the case will, as I understand, come before the Consular Court. There is every probability that the officers in question did not know a word of Arabic, as my servants do not know a word of English, to explain the position. My Arab stud manager is a most honourable, courteous, and trustworthy man, who has been many years with me, and it would be a great injustice to give him more than a nominal punishment for an offence which is due solely to his courage and fidelity in obeying an order given by me as a general one and without knowledge of special and unprecedented circumstances which have caused the collision.

    I have, &c.

        (Signed) WILFRID SCAWEN BLUNT

NO. 3.

The Marquess of Lansdowne to Sir R. Rodd.
(Telegraphic.)   Foreign Office, June 29, 1901

I HAVE received your telegram of the 23rd July.

    A long letter has reached me from Mr. W. Blunt. He states that he takes full responsibility for the action of his servants in the execution of his orders to them, which were not to allow any one within his walled garden on any pretence.

    Mr. Blunt appears to be especially anxious about what will happen to his Arab stud-groom. The case would, I presume, come in the ordinary course before the Native Tribunals, if it is decided to prosecute any of the men for assault.

NO. 4.

Sir R. Rodd to the Marquess of Lansdowne.—(Received July 30.)

(Telegraphic.)   Cairo, July 30, 1901

IN reply to your Lordship's telegram of yesterday, I have the honour to state that a report of the case was dispatched on the 25th July by post.

The three men charged with assault are being tried to-day before the ordinary Native Tribunal.

NO. 5.

Sir R. Rodd to the Marquess of Lansdowns.—(Received July 31).

(Telegraphic.)   Cairo, July 31, 1901

WITH reference to my telegram of yesterday, I have the honour to report that the Tribunal has given sentence in the case of Mr. Blunt's servants.

The stud-groom, Moutlak, was condemned to six months' imprisonment, and the other two accused to three and four months' respectively.

The defendants will probably appeal, and a lighter sentence may then be passed.

One of the pleas urged for the defence by the lawyer, who is also Mr. Blunt's steward, was that Mr. Blunt has given the strictest orders against trespassers; he stated that he had seen two Italians found on Mr. Blunt's property beaten with great severity.

NO. 6

Foreign Office to Mr Wilfrid Blunt

Sir,   Foreign Office, July 31, 1901

I AM directed by the Marquess of Lansdowne to acknowledge the receipt of your letter of the 25th instant on the subject of an incident which has arisen between some English fox-hunters and your servants near Cairo.

I am to state in reply that a copy of your letter will be forwarded to His Majesty's Acting Agent and Consul-General in Cairo, who has briefly reported the incident by telegraph, and from whom a detailed report is expected shortly.

I am, &c.

(signed) TH.SANDERSON.

P.S.—I am to add that a further telegram has been received from Sir R. Rodd, stating that the trial of your three servants was to take place on the 30th July before the ordinary Native Court.

NO. 7.

Foreign Office to Mr. Wilfrid Blunt.

Sir,   Foreign Office, July 31, 1901

WITH reference to my previous letter of to-day, I am directed by the Marquess of Lansdowne to inform you that a telegram has just been received from His Majesty's Acting Agent and Consul-General at Cairo reporting that the Egyptian Court has sentenced your stud-groom Moutlak to six months' imprisonment, and the two other defendants to four and three months' respectively.

Sir R. Rodd adds that the defendants will probably appeal, and that the sentence may then be reduced.

I am, &c.

(Signed) T.H. SANDERSON.

NO. 8.

Sir R. Rodd to the Marquess of Lansdowne.—(Received August 1)

My Lord,   Cairo, July 25, 1901

WITH reference to my telegram of the 23rd instant, I have the honour to transmit to your Lordship herewith copy of a Report made to the General Officer Commanding in Egypt by the Senior Officer present on the occasion of the assault made by Mr. Wilfrid Blunt's watchmen on some British officers on the 21st instant.

The result of an inquiry held yesterday has been that three of these employees of Mr. Blunt have been committed for trial.

The accused, in their deposition to the local police, stated that no assault had been committed by the officers, whom they only accused of trespass and damage to crops.

With regard to the latter point, the "procès-verbal de constantation", drawn up by the Parquet on the spot, shows that the damage inflicted was practically nil.

I have, &C.

(Signed) RENNELL RODD.

INCLOSURE IN NO. 8.

Major Rycroft to the Chief Staff Officer, Head-quarters, Cairo.

Sir,   Abbassiyeh, July 21, 1901

I BEG to report that the Abbassiyeh Fox Hounds met here this morning at 4 A.M.

The following officers went out with them:-

Major Rycroft, 11th Hussars.
Captain Greer, Mounted Infantry.
Captain Harman, A.C.S. (carrying the horn).
Lieutenant Rome, 11th Hussars (1st Whip).
Lieutenant Cayzer, 11th Hussars.
Lieutenant Buchanan, Seaforth Highlanders.
Lieutenant Hartwell, Leicester Regiment.
Private Bradley, 11th Hussars (2nd Whip)

We drew along the edge of the desert, and about 5 A.M. arrived outside the wall inclosing Mr. Wilfrid Blunt's property.

The hounds jumped the low wall, and immediately got on to the line of a fox, carrying it into the inclosure. Captain Harman and his two whips galloped for a hole in the wall, so as to get to their hounds, a Bedouin, whose name I afterwards ascertained to be Moutlak, shouting to them to stop, and striking at them with his stick.

I shouted in Arabic that they would do no harm,

but failing to stop them, the Bedouin summoned all the men of the place—Bedouins, ghaffirs, and syces—who, seizing sticks, followed Captain Harman and the others, the Bedouin Moutlak shouting to his followers to block all exits from the inclosure. I and the other officers remained outside, but hearing considerable shouting inside, we, after a few minutes, galloped back and entered the inclosure.

I found that both Captain Harman and Lieutenant Rome had been surrounded and mobbed, their hats knocked off, and they struck at, and their horses severely struck on heads and flanks, the ringleaders being Moutlak and a powerful grey-bearded ghaffir, by name Mohamed.

On arrival, I called these two to me, telling the officers to fall back, and promised to give my name, and to have the whole matter inquired into.

Moutlak was in a most excited state, and spoke most insolently. He, however, somewhat calmed himself, and we moved towards the entrance, Captain Harman calling on the hounds to follow.

As one hound was lagging behind, Lieutenant Hartwell and Lieutenant Cayzer turned back to bring him on, when the natives who were following picked up stones and clots of earth and pelted them, Mohamed, the ghaffir, rushing up and striking Lieutenant Hartwell across the back with a long and very thick stick, an Egyptian syce, clad in blue jersey and cord pants, at the same time striking Lieutenant Cayzer.

I called on Moutlak and Mohamed to order their

men to retire, and told the young officers not to strike back. We then all moved towards the Wakil's house (Hamoudah Effendi), but just before the latter appeared, Moutlak, the Bedouin, again became greatly excited, and rushed at one or two of the officers, poking at their horses' heads and eyes with his stick. On my expostulating with him, he rushed up, threatening to strike me, but thought better of it, and remained quiet. Hamoudah Effendi was most civil, and listened to the whole story, giving me the names I have quoted above, I at the same time giving him mine.

When the hounds jumped the wall and got on the line of a fox, it was necessary for the Master and Whips to be there, and not the slightest damage would have been done to crops.

As things turned out, it is possible that a small amount of damage may have been done, as perhaps three or four cotton-plants were trampled down, but chiefly by the natives when surrounding Captain Harman and Lieutenant Rome.

It is sincerely to be hoped that the chief offenders may be severely dealt with, as, unless the greatest forbearance had been exercised, the result must have been most serious.

There were in all from fifteen to twenty natives, mostly armed with thick sticks.

On behalf of the officers concerned, I wish to apologize to Mr. Blunt for any trespass that may have been committed, and need hardly say that we are willing to pay for any actual damage that may have been done to crops.

I have, &c.

> (Signed) W. RYCROFT, Major,
> Commanding 11th Hussads.

NO. 9.

Mr. Wilfrid Blunt to the Editor of the "Standard".

Sir,   Fernycroft, Beaulieu, Hants, August 4, 1901

THE wide publicity given in the "Standard" to the regrettable incident of Major Rycroft and his officers of the 11th Hussars and other regiments of the Cairo garrison having been assaulted and beaten by my native servants, while fox-hunting on my property near Cairo, obliges me to beg that you will courteously give space to the following statement of the facts supplementing and correcting the official résumé you have published.

I have owned land near Cairo for some twenty years. It consists of a house and large walled garden, standing formerly in the desert, but now surrounded with cultivated fields, irrigated from wells, and let in small holdings to peasant tenants. The garden itself was formerly a Khedival pleasance, and is highly cultivated with fruit trees, vegetables, and cotton. I pay 30s. an acre land tax for it, and it costs me £200. a year to keep up. Adjoining it, and inclosed in the same wall, 8 feet high, though on one side, where it is protected by a canal, somewhat lower, I have a second house and garden, where I keep my Arabian stud, the valuable brood-mares being tethered in it. I inhabit the place for four or five months every winter, and leave it in summer under the charge of trustworthy native servants. These have strict orders to allow no one during my absence within the inclosure except the gardeners, who live in the neighbouring villages, and who come to their work each morning. At night, according to custom, it is protected by an Arab guard under Government regulation. The whole is under the direction of a highly respectable Arab from Central Arabia, who manages my stud, and is responsible for order in the place. It is his special duty to see that the brood-mares are undisturbed, and that no strange stallion should approach them.

During my twenty years' ownership no violation of the garden has been attempted, except an occasional case of petty night marauding, or in the day-time of trespass by Greek or native vagabonds, easily expelled. As it is a very quiet place, with shade and water, it has become the resort and sanctuary of innumerable birds and not a few semi-wild four-footed beasts, which I take a pleasure in protecting. The officers of the 11th Hussars are known to me. Their Commanding Officer, Colonel Lumley, is a friend for whom I have a very high esteem, and who has been more than once my guest. He and they are well acquainted with the seclusion in which I live, and the seclusion of the place. I should have thought all of them bound by every honourable feeling to respect it in my absence. Nevertheless, it has been otherwise with certain of the officers. It appears that a few weeks ago these or others of the garrison brought from England a small pack of hounds, intending to introduce the sport of fox-hunting into Egypt, a country, I may say, entirely unsuited for it, and where it cannot but cause trouble with the natives, whose cultivation near Cairo is almost of a garden kind. I had heard nothing of this pack. No permission had been asked of me, or of any one in my service. There was no excuse of any kind for invading me, even on the most liberal interpretation of fox-hunting rights in England. It seems to have been on the part of the officers a kind of schoolboy frolic, and that they were unable to resist the temptation of blooding their hounds where they knew there were half-tame foxes handy. They chose what they must have thought a specially favourable moment. The Colonel of the 11th was away. The General in command of the English garrison was away. Lord Cromer was away. The hour, too, 5 o'clock on Sunday morning, was one apparently favourable to a little trespass. The garden-labourers would not be there, and the night-guard would have gone off duty. With a light heart, they proceeded to "draw my cover". Going to the lowest part of the wall, they put the hounds in, and Captain Harman, the master, and his two military whips of the Hussars followed, and presently found and, according to my advices, hunted and killed a fox inside the inclosure. It was not the act of sportsmen, but of boys—in itself a rather ill-bred proceeding, but not one which, if I had been there, I should have resented otherwise than by writing to their Colonels and begging that it should not be repeated.

With my servants it was otherwise. My stud-manager, seeing these horsemen galloping on their stallions through the place, got naturally indignant, and, when they refused to stop, called up the night-guard, which had not yet gone home. To put an end to the dangerous tomfoolery. According to the Arab's account, the officers struck the first blows with their riding-whips, and I think this is probable. Major Rycroft, in his Report, does not say clearly how this was: and it would be difficulty for the guards on foot to have struck the horsemen unless these had ridden at them. For my own part, although I deeply regret that servants of mine should under any provocation have found it necessary to lay hands on gentlemen holding His Majesty's commission, I can do no otherwise than acquit my servants of all blame. Indeed, I think they deserve the highest praise for their fidelity and courage. The officers were not in uniform, nor personally known to my people. They had no business whatever where they were or doing what they were doing, and were entitled to no consideration. At the outset, too, the officers must have been in superior numbers, and it was only when the gardeners began to arrive that the balance of strength turned the other way. Then Major Rycroft and his officers seem to have suddenly thought better of it, and effected a not very glorious retreat.

If the matter had ended there, there would have been no reason for my writing to you, or asking more publicity than the case has received. But it did not so end. Major Rycroft claims credit for his forbearance to having stopped his officers. In my opinion he would have acted a more manly and less ungenerous part by showing a little better and longer fight in a quarrel which he and his officers had brought upon themselves, than by revenging himself—as, in fact, he did. Allowing themselves to be overpowered by numbers (eight mounted English soldiers against no more than fifteen to twenty natives on foot), he and they capitulated—and then appealed to the law. In England, of course, such a solution of the difficulty would have been impossible. No Colonel of a regiment in his senses would sanction a summons for assault in like circumstances; and if he did, no Bench of Magistrates in the kingdom would hesitate to dismiss the case. But in Egypt the law is a quite different thing. In disputes between native and native there is, I think and hope, considerable improvement in the native Courts in the way of honest judgments, but between a native and an English officer things are still as bad as they ever were, and the conflict could not for an instant have been regarded as a fair one. It is to such a Court that Major Rycroft appealed in order, in his own words, that "the chief offenders should be severely dealt with", and with the inevitable result that he succeeded in having these worthy and courageous men, whom he and his officers had invited to a quarrel, so to say, on their own doorstep, sentenced to six and four and three months' imprisonment each.

If this is action worthy of the 11th Hussars, with their regiment's splendid traditions, the British Army has come, indeed, to a pretty pass. I hardly dare to add the last act in the affair, which gives it an almost comic touch. Major Rycroft and his officers, having been beaten on their backs, as they assert, by my servants, and taken their lawyer's revenge in Court, now write to me complaining of the bad language of my servants, and offering me a naïve apology.

I am, &c.

(Signed) WILFRID SCAWEN BLUNT.

NO. 10.
Sir R. Rodd to the Marquess of Lansdowne .—Received August 8.)
(Telegraphic.)   Cairo, August 8, 1901

ASSAULT on British officers.

At request of defendants' counsel, who urges domestic reasons, hearing of appeal has been postponed for a week.

NO. 11.
Sir R. Rodd to the Marquess of Lansdowne.—(Received August 12.)
My Lord,   Cairo, August 5, 1901

WITH reference to my despatch of the 25th ultimo, I have the honour to report that the Summary Court before which three employés of Mr. Wilfrid Blunt were tried for an assault on certain British officers, held that the charges as detailed in the report by Major Rycroft, inclosed in my despatch above referred to, were established, and sentenced the three offenders to terms of six, four, and three months' imprisonment respectively.

The public Prosecutor, in stating the case, anticipated the plea of defence that the responsibility for their action lay with their employer, saying that it was impossible to conceive that an English gentleman could have desired his servants to behave as they had done, and they could not, therefore, shift the blame on to his shoulders.

The counsel for the defence, Hamouda Effendi, replied that Mr. Blunt would certainly approve of their action, and stated in support of this contention that he had himself been an eye-witness of a case on the property, when two Italians who had trespassed were bound and beaten in Mr. Blunt's presence.

In reporting the case to your Lordship, I venture to draw attention to the fact that none of the officers present retaliated on their aggressors in spite of great provocation, and I think much credit is due to Major Rycroft, at the present time commanding the 11th Hussars, who exercised his authority with discretion. Had not the officers maintained the greatest self-restraint, very serious consequences might have ensued.

At the same time, comparing the sentences with those given in the Montazah affair last year, where the assault was of a very much graver character, I am of the opinion that they are somewhat unnecessarily severe. The defendants have appealed, and the appeal will be heard on the 8th instant, when I have little doubt there will be a considerable reduction in the sentences.

The incident appears to have taken place on the edge of some cultivated land by a cotton plantation; but the investigation went to show that practically no damage was done. It was explained to the Court that the trespass only occurred through the anxiety of the officers to remove the hounds immediately from Mr. Blunt's property.

I have not yet received a complete translation of the proceedings, but the above information has been supplied to me by one of the English Inspectors, under the Ministry of the Interior, who attended the trial.

I have, &c.

(Signed) RENNELL RODD.

NO. 12.

Mr. Wilfrid Blunt to the Marquess of Lansdowne.— (Received August 12.)

My Lord,   Clouds, Salisbury, August 10 1901.

SINCE writing to your Lordship on the 25th July, accounts have gradually reached me as to the unfortunate occurrence on my property at Sheykh Obeyd on the 21st. Among these the most important is a copy of the Official Report drawn up by Major Rycroft, commanding the 11th Hussars, and which your Lordship will doubtless have seen, together with a letter from that officer, both being dated the day of the occurrence. According to these it is evident that the entrance effected by the officers with their hounds was not, as Sir Thomas Sanderson suggested to me at the Foreign office, relying on a telegram, part of which he was good enough to read to me, from Sir Rennell Rodd, due to the accident of a fox, found outside, having taken refuge within my walled inclosure, but to the hounds having been brought to my garden and allowed to hunt there.

This will become clear to your Lordship if you will compare Major Rycroft's words with the inclosed rough plan of my Sheykh Obeyd Estate. [See frontispiece.]

Major Rycroft says: "We drew along the edge of the desert, and about 5 A..M. arrived outside the wall inclosing Mr. Wilfrid Blunt's property. The hounds jumped the low wall and immediately got on the line of a fox". This low wall can only have been that marked C C on the plan, the wall being there about 5 feet high, and low as compared with the rest of the inclosing line, whose average height is about 8 feet. It is the southern boundary of that portion of my garden which is appropriated to my Arab stud. Beyond it lies the second inclosure, marked A and B on the plan, which must be that indicated by Major Rycroft in the words "carrying it into the inclosure". Your Lordship will observe by the plan that the land outside the wall is also my property, divided from the inclosed portion only by a small canal, dry at this season of the year. The outer land, no less than the inner, is provided with notice boards warning off sportsmen, and inscribed, according to local custom, "Chasse réservée", with its equivalents in English and Arabic. It is, therefore, certain that the trespass was committed before the fox was found.

The intentional character, moreover, of the trespass is confirmed by the fact that Sheykh Obeyd lies 6 miles from Abbassiyeh, the head-quarters of the Hunt, and that, notwithstanding the distance, the Hunt arrived outside my wall at 5 A.M., an hour when it can have been hardly full daylight, so that, to arrive at my garden, they must have started in the dark. No master of hounds will gainsay the inference that, to travel with hounds 6 miles to a cover's edge, to arrive outside it at daylight, to encourage or allow hounds to leap the inclosing fence, the fence not being on a public road, to get on the line of a fox inside, and then to follow on horseback through the cover, proves an intention of drawing that cover, in other words of hunting in it.

Later, however, when the case was brought before Mr. Machell, the English adviser, and the Egyptian police authorities, with a view to my servants' arrest and prosecution, another complexion seems to have been put upon the affair. The intention of hunting, so clear in the first Report, was suppressed, and a theory of accidental trespass substituted. Thus Mr. Machell, writing to me on the 27th, speaks of the officers' intrusion as that of men "whose only desire was to get their hounds out of the inclosure", and Lord Cranborne, last Thursday in Parliament, gave as a reason that they rode inside "to prevent damage being done". Neither of these excuses is so much as hinted at in Major Rycroft's first Report, nor is it rational to believe that horsemen could have entered a garden to prevent damage, when the sole damage must have been that done by the horsemen themselves. Major Rycroft's words are quite different. Captain Harman, he says, and his whips entered "to get to their hounds", and again, "when the hounds jumped the wall and got on the line of a fox it was necessary for the Master and whips to be there". There is no suggestion whatever in these expressions of a desire to whip the hounds off, or get them out of the garden, rather of a desire to help them in their hunting. As a matter of fact, it native testimony is to count for anything, the officers hunted and killed a fox and a jackal inside the garden before their sport could be stopped.

Other points which I would press upon your Lordship's attention are:-

1. Major Rycroft's statement that stones were thrown at the officers—a statement repeated in Parliament by Lord Cranborne—cannot be correct. The soil of my garden is throughout of Nile mud and sand only, and contains no stones.

2. As to the damage done, Major Rycroft says: "It is possible that a small amount of damage may have been done, as perhaps three or four cotton plants were trampled down". The account given me on this head by my native tenant, who rents a portion of the land, and to whom the vegetable produce of the inner garden belonged, is as follows:-

Suleyman Effendi, writing on the 23rd July, says: "I have to inform your Excellency that the names here set down are those of some Englishmen who came and damaged the crops in the garden, both the cotton and the haricot beans (loubieh) of rather over 5 acres. Their dogs killed a fox and the she-jackal, and they themselves struck every one of our men who went to protest. Also I should wish to bring an action against them before the Mixed Tribunal claiming compensation for the damage. About this I await your reply and consent".

3. Major Rycroft, though he does not say it in words, implies that no blows were struck by the officers. It is impossible, however, to believe that this was the case. Independently of the native evidence, stands the fact that in an inclosure of over 70 acres the officers, should they have been approached, found themselves mounted opposed to men on foot and in so large a space they could have avoided a conflict had they so chosen. The native account just quoted is far more probable, that, on being expostulated with and told to stop, they rode at the guards, using their whips. How otherwise could they have been approached? The officers were probably surprised to find that instead of running away, as is usual in conflicts between Europeans and natives, these closed on them, seized their horses' bridles and roughly handled them. I feel certain that, except on the provocation of first blows received, no fellah and no Arab would have struck them. The object of the guard was to take their names and turn them out of the garden.

4. Major Rycroft complains of some of the officers having been beaten with sticks, yet as far as I can learn no wound or bruise has been produced in evidence, though such evidence is always required in the

native Courts. That they were roughly handled I do not doubt, but it was a case, I suspect, with them of having been "more frightened than hurt." Hamoudah Effendi Abdouh (who, be it noted, is not, as supposed at the Foreign Office, my steward or at all in my service, but a friend and neighbour, who being a lawyer did his best, when appealed to, to arrange the quarrel) thus sums up the matter. After relating (July 24) how the officers entered the garden with their hounds to hunt the foxes there and how Moutlak and the guard ejected them without, as they say, striking any blow, though some of the officers who had entered the garden affirm that they were beaten with sticks, and how he had called on the Major and officers afterwards on behalf of the servants to apologize, but without result, says: "The question has become a very grave one, and without your intervention the guards will be condemned. The guards were only doing their duty, but with a rather heavy hand." This probably describes the truth in a few words.

5. Moutlak, who, in Major Rycroft's Report, is spoken of only as a Bedouin, is in reality my stud manager, and sole manager of my garden during my absence. He receives the monthly sum from the Bank of Egypt, which he distributes in wages, and is alone responsible for order inside the inclosure. He has been in my service over ten years. On my leaving Egypt he received from me, as usual, the strictest orders to allow no one to enter either of the two inclosures except those employed in the work of the garden and stud— this for the double reason that it is necessary my

brood-mares should be undisturbed, and also to prevent the destruction of the garden's wild inhabitants, birds and beasts, of which it has been from all remembered time the asylum. He was only obeying my orders in using the force necessary to eject the intruders.

Having made these necessary observations on Major Rycroft's Report, I pass to the matter of the inadequacy of the native Courts to deal fairly with the case. For doubting the possibility of a just judgement in these courts Sir Thomas Sanderson took me gravely to task at the Foreign Office, and Lord Cranborne has stated since in Parliament that His Majesty's Government cannot interfere with the ordinary course of justice in the present instance, affirming that "the Egyptian Courts are as independent as the Courts of the United Kingdom and that it would be highly improper for His Majesty's Government to interfere with their discretion." All this may perhaps be true in theory, but in practice it is quite otherwise, as I think I can explain to your Lordship if you will do me the honour to listen to my reasons.

The Cadis, or County Court Judges, who try cases in the country districts, owe their appointments and all chance they have of promotion and increased pay to the good will of the English adviser of the Ministry of Justice indirectly to the English Agency, which, in fact though not in form, is the supreme authority in Egypt. In ordinary cases between native and native the Cadi knows that the English adviser wishes him to deal justly and that if he acts honestly and fearlessly he will be approved, whereas if he gives judgements corruptly or by favour he will be disapproved. In cases, however, where Englishmen are concerned there is in his mind no such certainly. He considers that an Englishman bringing a complaint before him is necessarily protected as such in some measure by the English authorities, and the balance of justice in his mind is from the outset disturbed. He gives his judgement in fear and trembling and almost always in the Englishman's favour. The Englishman's evidence is always accepted in the native Courts in preference to the native's evidence. In the present instance, where a number of English officers come before him declaring they have been assaulted and beaten, no possibility of an acquittal would find presence in the Cadi's mind. He knows that before the officers were allowed to bring their complaint into his Court, they must have obtained the approval, first, of the English General in command at Cairo, secondly, of the English Adviser of the Ministry of the Interior, thirdly, of the English Adviser of the Ministry of Justice, his own immediate superior, and fourthly, in a case of such great public scandal, of the English Agency. Thus fortified the case comes before him in his estimation already judged by all those on whose good will his prospects in life depend. He gives judgement with closed eyes, as he thinks will please them best. It is not necessary for the smallest pressure to be put upon him in the English officers' favour. The pressure is automatic. I assure your Lordship most earnestly that I do not exaggerate the case. When my servants were sentenced as they were (as I understand at Benha) they might just as well, for all their chance of acquittal, have gone before the Cadi undefended. Nor even I fear can it be much otherwise before the native Court of Appeal, superior in every way to the County Courts as the Appeal Court is. The case is too public a one and one too closely connected, if I may say so without being misunderstood, with the political status of the British occupation of Egypt, for it to be treated in an ordinary judicial spirit. Sir Rennell Rodd, in my opinion, and I think it will be the opinion of many besides myself, ought never to have allowed the case to be brought before the Courts, least of all before the native Courts, and His Majesty's Government cannot wash their hands of the injustice done except by further intervention in the direction of procuring the prisoners' pardon.

I urgently invite your Lordship to reconsider this important matter, as it is one that will certainly go far on men's tongues not only in Egypt, but throughout the East, and if unremedied will cause infinite discredit to the reputation of English justice.

I have, &c.

(Signed) WILFRID SCAWEN BLUNT

———————

NO. 13.

Sir R. Rodd to the Marquess of Lansdowne—(Received August 15.)

(Telegraphic.) Cairo, August 15, 1901

THE Court of Appeal has reduced the sentences on the men convicted of the assault on British officers from six, four, and three months, to two months, two months, and one month respectively. The Court declined to comply with an application from Mr. Blunt's lawyer for a further adjournment until a Report could be received from Mr. Blunt.

NO.14.

Foreign Office to Mr. Wilfrid Blunt.

Sir, Foreign Office, August 16, 1901

I AM directed by the Marquess of Lansdowne to acknowledge the receipt of your letter of the 10th instant relative to the assault committed by Egyptians in your service on a party of British officers near Cairo.

I am to inform you that a copy of your letter will be transmitted to His Majesty's Acting Agent and Consul-General at Cairo for his observations and for reference, if necessary, to the officers concerned.

I am, &c.

(Signed) T.H. SANDERSON

NO.15.

Foreign Office to Mr. Wilfrid Blunt.

Sir,   Foreign Office, August 16, 1901

I AM directed by the Marquess of Lansdowne to inform you that His Majesty's Acting Agent and Consul-General at Cairo reported by telegraph yesterday that the Court of Appeal has reduced the sentences passed on your servants from six, four, and three months' imprisonment to two months, two months, and one month respectively.

I am, &c.

(Signed) T.H. SANDERSON

NO.16.

War Office to Foreign Office—(Received August 17.)

Sir,   War Office, August 16, 1901

I AM director by the Secretary of State for War to forward herewith, for Lord Lansdowne's information, a copy of a telegram which has been received from the General Officer Commanding the forces in Egypt regarding the recent assault by Mr. Wilfrid Blunt's servants on some British officers.

I am, &c.

(Signed) E. W. D. WARD

INCLOSURE IN NO. 16.

General Officer Commanding in Egypt to Adjutant-General, London.

(Telegraphic.)   Cairo, August 14, 1901

I REPUDIATE entirely version given by Mr. Wilfrid Blunt in letter to "Standard," 6th August.

Official report by next mail.

NO. 17.

Sir R. Rodd to the Marquess of Lansdowne.—(Received August 19.)

My Lord,   Cairo, August 12, 1901

WITH reference to my despatch of the 5th instant, I have the honour to transmit to your Lordship herewith a summary of the evidence given at the trial of Mr. Wilfrid Blunt's servants for an assault on some officers who had entered Mr. Blunt's property to call off their fox-hounds, which had jumped over the wall of the inclosure.

I also inclose a note by Captain Hopkinson, who was present at the trial on behalf of the Ministry of the Interior, on a statement made by the counsel of the defendants in Court with regard to the treatment which trespassers on the property had received on a former occasion.

The proceedings in this case have been perfectly regular. The Parquet conducted a preliminary investigation, and then instituted a prosecution before the Summary Court at Benha on the 30th ultimo. Against the Judgement the defendants have appealed, and the appeal was adjourned at the request of Mr. Blunt's lawyer, on the plea of the illness of his mother. It will be tried on the 15th instant.

I had already reported to your Lordship the main

facts of the case, and should not have had much to add to my previous reports were it not that, a few hours ago, I received the English papers of the 6th instant, and my attention has been drawn to a letter from Mr. Blunt in the "Standard" of that date which I cannot pass over without certain observations.

Before entering into any details, I would mention that, immediately after the occurrence of the incident, Major Rycroft, as the senior officer present, sent a letter to Mr. Blunt, inclosing a copy of the report made by him to the General Officer Commanding in Egypt, that he might be in possession of the facts of the case, and, at the same time, expressing his regret that such an incident had taken place on his property. The use which Mr. Blunt makes of this comunication in the concluding paragraph of his letter may do credit to his skill as an ingenious controversialist, but is otherwise scarcely worthy of his pen.

I will pass over the insinuations implied in the third paragraph of his letter, of a deliberate intention to "flesh" a newly-arrived pack of hounds on the half-tame foxes of a well-known protector of animals during the absence of the Colonel of the regiment and other superior authorities, merely observing that the hounds in question have been some time in Egypt, and that they have constantly been taken out across the desert in the direction of Birket-el-Haj, some miles beyond Mr. Blunt's property, in the presence of the Colonel himself, for more than two months before the incident occurred.

But the concluding words of the paragraph in question cannot be so easily passed over.

On the morning of the 21st July the hounds met at 4 a.m., and started to proceed in the same direction—towards Birket-el-Haj. The way lay along the edge of the desert, and thus passed between the wall of Mr. Blunt's property and a dry canal. It was while passing along this wall that the hounds winded a fox and jumped over the wall.

Mr. Blunt writes:-

"With a light heart, they proceeded to 'draw my cover.' Going to the lowest part of the wall, they put the hounds in, and Captain Harman, the master, and his two military whips, of the Hussars, followed, and presently found, and, according to my advices, hunted, and killed a fox inside the inclosure."

These statements I venture to traverse, both on the grounds of the sworn evidence collected by the Parquet and from the statements I have myself received from those who were present.

There was no intention to trespass on Mr. Blunt's property. They did not "put the hounds in." They did not hunt and kill a fox in his grounds. Seeing, however, that the hounds had jumped the wall on a scent, those responsible did their best to withdraw them without delay. With this object, Captain Harman and the two ships rode on along the wall until they came to a gap, into which they turned to call the hounds off. It was here, I am informed, that they were first opposed and struck at by the Bedouin, Moutlak.

Mr. Blunt, however, writes that his stud manager, "seeing these horsemen galloping their stallions through the place, got indignant." This is not consistent with the statement that they were first struck at while turning in through the gap in the wall. The rest of the officers halted some distance outside the inclosure, thus showing that there was no intention of hunting inside, while Major Rycroft endeavoured to appease the violence of Moutlak by explaining what had occurred.

It was only some time afterwards, when the three who had gone in were surrounded and struck by a number of men, that the others went in.

It is untrue, on the evidence of the sworn testimony, that the officers struck the first blows with their riding whips, probable though it appears to Mr. Blunt. They were, moreover, not in superior numbers, for there were only three horsemen inside until the moment when Major Rycroft and his brother officers, thinking the position critical, went in to their support. The fact that certain blows were struck on their backs, which Mr. Blunt finds suggestive, was due to the fact that the "worthy and courageous men" who were surrounding them probably thought it safest to strike from behind. They appear also to have devoted equal, if not more, energy to striking the horses.

It is not necessary for me to discuss the insinuations implied in such phrases as "allowing themselves to be overpowered by numbers…. they capitulated and appealed to the law," or again, "he would have acted a more manly and less ungenerous part in showing a little better and longer fight." The intention of such insinuations is obvious. Major Rycroft acted, in every respect, in the spirit of the general instructions which regulate the conduct of the British forces in Egypt, and it is certainly due to his discretion, under great provocation, in preventing any act of retaliation, that very serious consequences did not ensue.

Mr. Blunt, it would appear, advocates taking the law into ones own hands, and the statement made by his own counsel as to the treatment accorded by him to the humbler class of sportsmen, shows that such are the principles which he inculcates on his servants, who seem, in this case, to have been rather the victims of their instructions. It is undoubtedly fortunate that the officers, whom they assaulted were better advised.

In conclusion, I would only observe that Major Rycroft, on whom Mr. Blunt has made a personal attack, wholly unwarranted, I venture to think, by the facts of the case, confined his action to laying the matter before the General Officer Commanding in Egypt, the only course open to him.

I have expressed to Major Rycroft my approval of the wise discretion which he exercised, in preventing any act of retaliation. He has already expressed his regrets for the involuntary trespass which occurred.

I have, &c.

(Signed) RENNELL RODD

INCLOSURE 1 IN NO. 17.

Summary of Evidence given at the Trial of Mr. Wilfrid Blunt's Servants for an Assault on British Officers.

THE Summary Court for the trial of délits was held at Benha on Tuesday, the 30th July, 1901, for the trial of the case recorded under No. 21 (Saira), in the Parquet's list, and under No. 540 on the court Roll of 1901.

Present:

Faud Bey Brais, President.

Abdul Megid Bey Radwan, Chef du Parquet of Cairo; and

Ibrahim Effendi Sherif, Clerk.

The proceedings were public.

Versus –

1. Moutlak Bital, Bedouin, 40 years of age, head syce by occupation, living at Ain-el-Shems;

2. Mohammed Ramadan, 50 years of age, a gaffir, living at El Khassoos;

3. Mohammed Omar, 28 years of age, syce, living at El Marg.

(The above were imprisoned on July 25, 1901.)

The accused are charged with the offence of having formed themselves into a band of more than five persons, and of having assaulted Lieutenants Cayzer and Hartwell, and Private Bradley, of the British Army of Occupation, on the 21st July last.

The accused, with Hamouda Effendi Abdou, their advocate, were brought before the Court, as well as the witnesses in the case. The interpreter (Habeeb Effendi) was also present.

The Chef du Parquet explained to the Court that the persons above charged had surrounded and struck Lieutenants Cayzer and Hartwell, and Private Bradley, on the 21st July last, and demanded that they should be punished in accordance with Article 220 of the Penal Code (last paragraph).

The accused, being questioned, denied having committed the offence, and Mohammed Omar alleged that he had been struck with a whip by one of the complainants.

Habeeb Effendi Kamel, interpreter, 25 years of age, having been sworn, was directed to translate to the Court the statements of the witnesses.

Witness, Major Rycroft, Commanding 11th Hussars, Abbassia, being sworn, was questioned, and stated as follows:-

On the 21st July last I and certain officers went out hunting. We left Abbassia at 4 A.M.., Captain Harman and Lieutenant Rome (the 1st whip), with Private Bradley in the hunt. After about an hour's ride along the canal near the desert, we reached a spot adjacent to the house of Mr. Blunt. It was then about 5 A.M. Suddenly the hounds jumped over the wall of the garden. From the movements of the latter the officers concluded that the hounds had found a fox. The hounds afterwards passed through some culti-vated land, which I knew to be the property of Mr. Blunt (for I am acquainted with this part of the coun-try). The hounds then jumped over the wall of the garden which is about as high as this (indicating with his hand a height of about 1½ metres). There was a door in the wall inclosing the land, but it was closed. At a short distance from it there is an opening in the wall about as long as this table (i.e., from 4 to 5 metres long). Captain Harman and his companions and Private Bradley walked along the wall, and passed the door which was shut. They, however, entered by the opening in the wall with the object of calling back the hounds, which had entered Mr. Blunt's property.

The other officers waited, not wishing to enter. While I was waiting outside, I saw this bedouin (pointing out Moutlak) coming from the direction of the stables. He entered by the opening in the wall. He was carrying a stick. He called out to his companions. They approached the officers, as if they meant to assault them. I was at a distance of 70 yards from them. I told Moutlak, in Arabic (which I can speak a little) that there was nothing wrong; that no harm would be done. Moutlak said to his companions something to the effect that they would close all exits. About seven or eight persons, who had come from the same direction as Moutlak, followed up the latter.

About five minutes after the officers had gone inside I heard shouting, and concluding that something had gone wrong I was obliged to enter the enclosure., I went towards Captain Harman, taking the same path that he had followed (i.e., through a part of the ground which was not cultivated). Lieutenant Rome hastened towards me; he was hatless. He informed me that the men in question knocked off his hat and threatened to strike him. On proceeding further I found Captain Harman hatless as well, and surrounded by a larger number of natives than those who had accompanied the Bedouin at first. They had with them long sticks. Captain Harman informed me that these men having surrounded him, struck his horse, causing his hat to fall off, and further had attempted to strike him. As far as I can remember these men numbered from fifteen to twenty, or even more. They were in a most excited state, shouting and raising their sticks. They threatened to strike us.

The ringleaders were Moutla and Mohammed, for they were more conspicuous by their shouting and threatening. I approached the persons who were gathered together and asked them to be quiet. I then called to me Moutlak and Mohammed. As to the rest of the officers, they stood at 15 yards from me, except Captain Harman, who was waiting with the hounds in a spot which is not cultivated. I remember that when Moutlak approached me he was holding a hat or perhaps two. I spoke to him in Arabic in a manner which he could understand, telling him that we were officers of the Army of Occupation, and that I was the officer commanding the troops at Abbassia, and that the fact that we were not in our uniforms (except Private Bradley) made no difference.

Moutlak replied that he did not care a bit about that, as he doubted my statement. He was much excited, and pointing at Captain Harman, said he (Captain Harman) was not an officer, but a Soudanese syce. Though Moutlak was very excited, and spoke in an insolent manner, the other officers remained silent. Eventually I asked him to give me the names of his men, and to bring me a pencil and some paper. In turn I promised to give him my name and the names of the other officers. He then calmed down, and afterwards we passed out by the same opening in the wall.

None of us passed over the cultivated land, but I noticed that many of the persons who had collected together passed through the cotton plantation, so that some shrubs were bent down. None of the officers, however, passed through it. On our passing through the opening in the wall two officers were on my left hand and the rest behind me. Moutlak was near me, but Mohammed, a gaffir, was in front of the crowd of people, with a long stick in the hand. Having again heard shouting, I turned round and saw two of the officers who had lagged behind me return to the spot where we were. They were followed by a large number of men with sticks raised in their hands. I called out to the officers, and told Moutlak to prevent his men from striking any one. He did so, but when the officer came near me, they informed me that they had returned to find a hound which had gone astray. While doing so the natives attacked them, one dealing Lieutenant Hartwell a severe blow on the back. Another man, Mohammed Omar by name, struck Lieutenant Cayzer. Thereupon I said to Moutlak that I would not quit the place unless their names were given me. I asked for a pencil and paper, and waited for some time, but no pencil or paper was brought. I then asked Moutlak to give me his own name. Moutlak said that he was called "the Wekil of Mr. Blunt [sic]. His men also said most insolently that they all named "Blunt". Having expressed a wish to go to the Wekil's house, one of them pointed it out. It was situated at a distance of 300 yards. It was then late in the day. In passing through the opening in the wall to proceed to the Wekil's house the gaffir seized the reins of my horse, and when I asked him to drop them he shook the reins. Three officers had then gone out, but the others were coming behind me. On their passing through the opening the crowd opposed them, and attempted to prevent them proceeding.

Lieutenant Hartwell informed me that these men had pelted him and the other officers with clods of earth. When we got outside the wall I was told that the Wekil, Hamouda Effendi, was coming, so I went to meet him. Before reaching the house of the latter I saw one of the officers pursuing a syce, and saw Moutlak with a stick in his hands. He was in an excited state, and began to strike the officer's horse on the head. This occurred just as we came near to the house of Hamuda Effendi. When I asked Moutlak to desist, he raised his stick and attempted to strike me, but did not actually do so. Mohammed then seized the reins of my horse to prevent me proceeding any further. I told them that I would not quit the place.

As Hamouda Effendi then came out I informed him in French of the occurrence. I gave him my name and the names of the other officers. Hamuda

Effendi was very polite, and gave me his name . I told him that the officers were compelled to enter the garden to control the hounds, but that I and the other officers only entered when we heard shouting inside. I explained to him how Moutlak misbehaved towards us, and that he and his men called themselves "Blunt", &c. Finally, I pointed out to him that Mr. Blunt or any other person was amenable to the law.

Q. To the Witness: Do you know how Lieutenant Hartwell and Lieutenant Cayzer were struck? —A.. Lieutenant Hartwell told me that Mohammed Ramadan had dealt him a severe blow on the back with a long stick, causing him great pain. Lieutenant Hartwell wished to return to strike his assailant, but I prevented him from doing so. I was informed by Lieutenant Cayzer that his man (pointing out a certain syce) had struck him. I did not see the blow given.

Q. Were there any traces of the blow?—A. No.

Q. By Hamuda Effendi to Witness: Can you describe the field, the property of Mr. Blunt?—A. Yes; I know the place. When you enter by the opening in the wall, you come to the stables for the horses, the other side is an open space. I entered quietly in order not to disturb the horses. I have known for some time that the place belongs to Mr. Blunt, but there was no objection to entering for hunting purposes (i.e., there were no instructions forbidding entrance). I admit, however, that there is a sign-board on which is inscribed that hunting is prohibited. This sign-board is fixed on the side of the road leading to Hamouda

Effendi's house. It is an open space, so one cannot decide whether this prohibition refers to the property belonging to Mr. Blunt or to that of Hamouda Effendi.

Q. What is the position of the sign-board?—A. On the road. One cannot see it unless one is passing by the house of Hamuda Effendi.

Q. Was there no house belonging to Mr. Blunt opposite the stables?—A. The house in which Mr. Blunt lives is at 400 yards distant. However, owing to some trees, one cannot see it. Perhaps there is a house there, for there are some buildings on the spot.

(Signed) W. RYCROFT, Major, 11th Hussars.

Benha, July 30, 1901.

Sir Brodrick Hartwell, Lieutenant, British Army, living at Abbassieh, on being sworn, stated as follows:-

Q. Can you tell me who struck you?—A. I do not know his name (pointing out Mohamed Ramadan), but Moutlak struck my horse.

Q. How did Mohamed Ramadan strike you?— A. I had returned to bring up a hound that was lagging behind, and was surprised to be surrounded by five or six persons, one of whom struck me with a nabout on the back. I turned round and saw Mohamed Ramadan.

Q. Did the blow leave any marks?—A. No.

Q. Was it a severe blow?—A. It caused me great pain.

Q. How did Moutlak strike your horse?—A. Moutlak struck my horse with a nabout, between the eyes. This took place while we were waiting before the house of Hamuda Effendi, in order to communicate the matter to him.

Q. Why did he do this?—A. I do not know; but he was very excited, and was insulting me.

Q. How do you know that he was insulting you?—A. I understand that the word "dog" is an insult in Arabic.

Q. Did you see any of the accused strike any one besides yourself?—A. I saw Moutlak approach the Major and seize hold of his bridle, and I saw the syce strike at the officers when they were leaving through the opening in the wall.

Q. By the Parquet: Did you not see who struck Lieutenant Cayzer?—A. I heard that he was struck, but did not see who struck him.

Q. By Hamuda Effendi: At what time did you receive the blow?—A. When I had returned back to find the hound which had strayed.

Q. By the Court: Did they strike you in order to prevent you re-entering?—A. We had not yet left, and I had turned and was proceeding to find out where the hound was.

Q. By the Lawyer: Who went with you to find the hound?—A. I had started alone, but Lieutenant Cayzer turned his horse towards me.

Q. Do you remember if Lieutenant Cayzer was struck at the same time that you were assaulted, or before or after you?—A. I cannot tell.

(Signed) BRODERICK HARTWELL,
Lieutenant.

Lieutenant Cayzer, aged 19 years, Lieutenant, British Army, having been sworn, stated as follows:-

Q. Who struck you?—A. Mohamed Omar, Syce.

Q. With what?—A. A thorny stick.

Q. On what part of the body did the blow fall?—A. On my right arm.

Q. Did the blow leave traces?—A. No.

Q. Describe the circumstances under which the blow was inflicted.—A. While endeavouring to prevent me going out by the opening in the wall, he struck me.

Q. Did you see any of the accused strike any one besides yourself?—A. I saw Mohamed Ramadan strike Lieutenant Hartwell with a stick on the back; the Bedouin struck Lieutenant Hartwell's horse on the forehead.

Q. Did your hat fall off accidentally, or because some one knocked it off?—A. My hat did not fall off.

Q. By the Lawyer: Did you return with Lieutenant Hartwell?—A. I returned when I saw the men attacking him.

Q. Did you see him then, when he was struck?—A. Oh, yes; saw him when he was struck with a stick on the back.

(Signed) CAYZER, Lieutenant.

Private William Bradley, aged 19 years, British Army, was sworn, and stated as follows:-

Q. Who struck you?—A. In answering, Bradley pointed out Moutlak, taking hold of the latter's arm, and said: It is this man who struck me.

Q. On what part of the body did he strike you?—A. He struck me on the shoulder with a long stick.

Q. Are there any marks left on your body?—A. No.

Q. Do you know why he (Moutlak) struck you?—A. When I entered the inclosure to call back the hounds, the men pelted me with clods of earth; Moutlak struck me with a stick on the shoulder; moreover, some other persons who were standing under the trees pelted me with clods of earth.

Q. Did you see any of the accused strike any one besides yourself?—A. I saw Lieutenant Cayzer riding after one of them.

Q. After whom?—A. In answering this question, Bradley pointed out Mohamed Omar.

Q. Did you know why Lieutenant Cayzer ran after the said man?—A. No.

Q. Have you heard that Lieutenant Cayzer was struck?—A. Yes, I have heard so.

Q. By the Parquet: Did not Moutlak strike you with a brick (sic)—A. He pelted me with a clod of earth, which struck my side. (Here the Chef du Parquet showed the whip to Private Bradley, which the latter identified and stated that it was his.)

Q. By the Lawyer: Did you inform the Major that you had been struck?—A. I at first informed Lieutenant Rome, and he informed the Major.

(Signed) BRADLEY.

Lieutenant Rome, having been summoned, was sworn. He stated he was aged 22 years, and a

Lieutenant in the British Army. When questioned as to what he had seen of the affair, he stated as follows:-

On Sunday, the 21st July last we went out hunting. As the hounds entered the garden belonging to Mr. Blunt, we followed them to call them back. Thereupon the natives threatened us, and Mahomed, a gaffir, attacked me. A man with a beard struck a horse with his nabout (pointing at Mahomed Ramadan); afterwards I returned to the garden with Major Rycroft. I saw one of the men seize hold of the reins of the horse belonging to Captain Harman. There was much shouting and disturbance. Afterwards we left the garden and proceeded to the house of the Wekil. We gave the latter our names, and he also, in turn, gave us the names of his men.

Q. By the Court: How did your hat fall off?—A. It fell off while I was passing under some trees on my way back.

(Signed) LESLIE ROME

Statement of the Chef du Parquet.

When the statements of the officers concerned were taken down, the Chef du Parquet explained the particulars of the case, a précis of which is as follows:

On the 21st July last seven officers and a soldier went out hunting. They arrived at Ain-el-Shems (Helopolis), where the property of Mr. Blunt is situated. This measures about 2,100 metres. It is surrounded by a mud wall roughly constructed. He then described the garden, and pointed out where the house belonging to Mr. Blunt was situated, as well as a plot of land leased to a certain Suleiman Effendi, and sown with cotton. The hounds, when following the fox, jumped over the wall. Some of the officers were obliged to enter in order to control the hounds, knowing that there were some gazelles kept inside belonging to Mr. Blunt. When Moutlak saw this, he fetched a stick, calling the rest of the servants, who came armed with nabouts. Major Rycroft, who was waiting outside, noticed that Moutlak was in an excited state, and fearing serious consequences he saw also obliged to enter to see what was the matter. Here the Chef du Parquet describes the disturbance caused by Moutlak and his men: one of them (Mohamed Ramadan) dealing Lieutenant Hartwell two blows with a stick; one struck the horse which caused Captain Harman's hat to fall off.

Major Rycroft tried to appease Moutlak and his men, but his endeavours were futile. He informed them that he and the others were British officers. Moutlak, pointing at Captain Harman, said that the latter was meaner than a Soudanese Syce; they spoke insolently to the officers, whereas had they followed the example of their master, Mr. Blunt, they would have received the officers with respect and rendered the necessary assistance. The accused denied having committed any assault, or that they behaved improperly towards the officers. If this were really true, the officers would not have deposed before the Court that they had been struck. Moreover, a certain Suleiman in the employ of Mr. Blunt testified that he saw Moutlak strike the officers with a stick. It was also proved from the evidence of a certain Abd Rabboh that the officers were assaulted.

The land which belongs to Mr. Blunt is uncultivated, and even had the officers damaged the cotton plantation, Moutlak and his men should not have interfered, for the cotton crop belongs to Suleiman Effendi Idrees, and it was therefore the duty of the latter's servants to attend to the matter. But the fact that these servants (of Suleiman Effendi) did not take any part in the affair proves that no damage whatever occurred. Further, from the "constation" when the Mudir of Kalioubia was present, no damage to the cotton plantation was proved, except that a few plants had been trodden down. Assuming that Moutlak and his companions were protecting the property of their employer, why should Moutlak seize the reins of the horse of Major Rycroft when the latter was leaving the place?

Why should Moutlak and his men assault some of the officers when they were outside the inclosure when the officers had used no force whatever towards their assailants? These men committed these acts simply because they are bad characters and unprincipled persons.

The Chef du Parquet, after pointing out the fact that blows were inflicted on the officers inside the inclosure as well as outside, proceeded to explain the false statement of Mohamed Omar, who alleged that he had been beaten. The latter produced a whip which, he said, he had succeeded in taking from one of the officers. The medical examination proved that the marks on the body of Mohamed Omar were not inflicted by a whip, but possibly by a stick. Private Bradley declared that he had lost his whip during the affray. Mohamed Omar, who found it, alleged that he took it when he was beaten. Moreover, he (Mohamed Omar) did not assert that Bradley had struck him.

The Chef du Parquet pointed out that Moutlak was the principal instigator, and he had attempted to strike Major Rycroft without any motive, and therefore deserves a severe punishment.

Mohamed Ramadan more than once struck Lieutenant Hartwell and the horse of Mr. Rome, inside and outside the inclosure, although he was not so furious as Moutlak.

Mohamed Omar, who also assaulted some of the officers, was recognized by the latter from his dress—i.e., a blue jersey and cord pants.

As to the officers, their conduct was correct, and they had not assaulted any of the accused, who confessed this fact. Had the officers defended themselves against the assaults they would have suffered more serious injury.

In conclusion, the Chef du Parquet demanded that the accused be severely dealt with in accordance with Article 220, Penal Code, last paragraph, especially as regards their ringleader.

The Defence made by Hamouda Effendi Abdou on behalf of the accused.

In defending the accused, Hamouda Effendi asked that he might be excused for demanding that the accused be acquitted. English officers are upholders of the law, and, therefore, desire to see justice administered to all without partiality.

In the report submitted by Major Rycroft, it is stated that, on reaching Mr. Blunt's property, the hounds entered the inclosure. When the officers followed them, the accused endeavoured to prevent them proceeding further.

They conducted them to my house, and the affair ended there. The officers have no evidence to prove that the accused struck them, except presumptive evidence.

The officers alleged that their hats were knocked off by the accused, whereas it appeared that a hat fell down, the owner having brushed against a tree; another hat, worn by an officer on horseback, also fell off when the horse became restive. The complainants describe the sticks as being long ones. If such were the case, they must have left traces on the bodes of the persons beaten. Mohamed Omar (one of the accused), who stated before the police that he was beaten by one of the officers, bore at the time traces of blows on his body; but the Parquet did not inquire into the case until three days after the occurrence, and all traces had then disappeared.

It was proved from the "constation" that the crops of half a feddan was damaged, having been trampled down under the feet of the horses. Also, Major Rycroft, in concluding his report, stated as follows:-

"On behalf of the officers concerned, I apologize to Mr. Blunt, and we are ready to pay for any damage that may have been done to the crops".

This declaration is a sufficient motive for the acquittal of the accused.

The Parquet asked that the accused be condemned in accordance with Article 220, Penal Code. This Article is not applicable to the case in question, neither is the Decree issued as a supplement to the said Article. Hamouda Effendi said that in accordance with Article 220, Penal Code, the accused are excusable, and that Article 229 is applicable in this case.

It is well known that Mr. Blunt bought his garden from Saced Pasha. This property is neither sand nor desert, for Mr. Blunt has added to it 40 feddans whereon he has built a house, stables, and stores, and the property therefore comes under the definition of Article 226. It was on these premises that the incident occurred. Now, in accordance with Article 390 of the French Code, the garden is considered as an inhabited place (here Hamouda Effendi read the said Article in French and translated it into Arabic).

There were on the spot stables and stores, the keys of which he kept, &c.; the place could not be described as a desert; any building surrounded by a wall as well as a garden is considered as annexes to the house itself.

Hamouda Effendi proceeded to explain Article 226, and said that the latter part of it is applicable to this case; but the latter part referred him to Article 229 (which he read over to the Court) and he then referred to Article 220. If this Article 220, Penal Code, is applicable to the affair in question the Decree which prescribes a punishment of three years (being a supplement to the said Decree) must also be made applicable to this case.

The Court is aware that the said Decree was intended to prevent individuals of bad character forming a band and making attacks on peaceable persons. A previous agreement must be arrived at between the individuals composing the band, and the latter must comprise five members.

The said conditions stipulated by the said Decree were not fulfilled in this case, and therefore it cannot be made applicable to this case, the accused being three only.

It follows that Article 220, together with Article 229, will have to be applied to this case, and, according to the latter, the accused might be considered excusable in their dealings with the officers.

In conclusion, Hamouda Effendi contended that the accused were fully excusable in view of the fact that Mr. Blunt took special interest in his garden and wished to keep it always in good condition, and would not allow any one to enter it, and is particularly fond of it and the animals kept therein. He has published his views in a book which is read by English people. Mr. Blunt was of opinion that wild animals will not injure a man unless he attacks them. The accused, therefore, were obliged to prevent the officers entering the property, especially so, when it is considered that the officers would cause damage to the garden and to the crops of half a feddan of cotton plantation. In their endeavours to prevent the officers, the accused were only performing their duty towards their master.

Finally, Hamouda Effendi expressed the hope that the officers would pardon the accused, but left the matter to the discretion of the Court.

The Court, after hearing the statements of all concerned, sentenced the accused to six, four, and three months' imprisonment respectively, and costs, the period during which they were in custody pending trial being deducted from the term of imprisonment, in accordance with Article 220, Penal Code, paragraph 1.

INCLOSURE 2 IN NO. 17.

Note by Captain Hopkinson.

I WAS present during the whole of this trial. In the speech made by Hamouda Effendi Abdou for the defence, he drew attention to a statement made by the Chef du Parquet that "Mr. Blunt would have treated the officers with respect". This statement he questioned. He further related, in disproof of this, and to show how particular Mr. Blunt was about trespass, that, on a certain occasion, he was present in Mr. Blunt's garden, that some Italians entered to shoot, that they were seized by Mr. Blunt's servants, that their hands bound, and were severely beaten; that Mr. Blunt was present, and asked him what he should do with them, and that he advised him to release them. After the trial I expressed surprise to Hamouda Effendi that he should have said such a thing. He replied. "I said it because it happened, and I was an eye-witness of it".

> (Signed) H. HOPKINSON, Captain,
> Inspector, Ministry of the Interior.
> Cairo, August 11, 1901.

NO. 18.
Sir R. Rodd to the Marquess of Lansdowne.—(Received August 19.)

My Lord,   Cairo, August 13, 1901

WITH reference to my immediately preceding despatch, I have the honour to report that the appeal of the defendants, condemned for an assault on some British officers on Mr. Blunt's property, should have been heard on the 8th instant. Mr. Blunt's lawyer, however, asked for, and obtained, an adjournment of a week on the somewhat unusual plea of his mother's illness. About the same time the native papers published paragraphs announcing the impending intervention of the British Foreign Office.

I have, &c.

> (Signed) RENNELL RODD.

NO. 19.
Sir R. Rodd to the Marquess of Lansdowne.—(Received August 19.)

(Telegraphic.)   Cairo, August 19, 1901

ASSAULT on officers.

In my telegraph of the 15th August please read "two months, one month, and one month", for "two months, two months, and one month".

NO. 20.

Foreign Office to Mr. Wilfrid Blunt.

Sir, Foreign Office, August 19, 1901. WITH reference to my letter of the 16th instant, I am directed by the Marquess of Lansdowne to inform you that he has to-day received a telegram from His Majesty's Agent and Consul-General at Cairo, stating that the Court of Appeal reduced the sentences on your servants for assaulting a party of British officers to two months, one month, and one month respectively, and not to two months, two months, and one month as stated in his previous telegram I am, &c.

(Signed) T. H. SANDERSON.

NO. 21

Mr. Wilfrid Blunt to Viscount Cranborne.—(Received August 22.)

My Lord,   August 17, 1901

WITH reference to Sir Charles Cayzer's question asked in Parliament on Thursday and your Lordship's answer, I beg to inform you that there is no truth in the story referred to, namely, that two Greeks found trespassing in my garden in Egypt were at any time flogged by my direction until they were insensible, or, according to your Lordship's version, that two Italians were bound and severely beaten in my presence.

During my twenty years' ownership of Sheykh Obeyd, a few, perhaps half-a-dozen, cases have occurred of quarrel with trespassers, generally Greek gunners in pursuit of small birds, or of such being ejected from the premises; but in no instance that I can remember has undue violence been used by my servants, nor has complaint ever been lodged against them till now in any Court. On the contrary, such quarrels have been unimportant and have, I believe in every instance, ended by the intruders acknowledging themselves in the wrong, desisting from their trespass, and apologizing. This is the more remarkable when it is considered that during the greater part of this long period the district immediately surrounding my property has borne a notoriously bad character, and was for some years a centre of organized brigandage.

The only instance which has come to my knowledge of Europeans having been perhaps too roughly treated by my servants was not a case of ordinary trespass, but of four men being found after sunset with arms inside my inclosure, a circumstance of suspicion which might have subjected them to criminal proceedings. They were by my orders arrested and detained till the police could take cognizance of the case, and two of them received a somewhat severe handling while resisting capture. They were not, as far as I remember, bound, and certainly were not flogged or beaten after being secured, while, so far from lodging complaint against me with the police when they arrived, they expressed deep gratitude to me for accepting their excuses and not pressing the case against them. It is probably to this incident, which happened a year or two ago, that the counsel quoted by your Lordship referred (if, indeed, his words were accurately reported) in the exaggerated terms which have reached His Majesty's Government.

I will ask your Lordship to take an early opportunity, if possible before the Session closes, of communicating to the House of Commons my denial of Sir Charles Cayzer's malevolent story, as well as of the revised tale as suggested to the House by your Lordship's official statement.

It is a misfortune of the country districts of Egypt that in spite of recent police improvements they are still too little protected by the law to make it possible to dispense with the old-fashioned custom of employing Arab guards wherever there is valuable property to protect. I should personally be most glad to be relieved from the burden of this necessity, which is both irksome and costly, but, while the Executive remains as weak as it is against lawlessness, especially European lawlessness, everyone living outside the towns has, so to speak, in the first instance to defend his own head.

I am, &c.

(Signed) WILFRID SCAWEN BLUNT

NO. 22.

Sir R. Rodd to the Marquess of Lansdowne. —(Received August 26.)

My Lord,   Cairo, August 19, 1901.

WITH reference to previous correspondence respecting the assault on some British officers by Mr. Wilfrid Blunt's servants, I have the honour to report that the episode appears to have created a generally favourable impression among the natives, who are, I am informed, much struck by the correct attitude of the officers, in simply appealing to the law, and refraining from any acts of reprisal or violence. The sentences, as reduced by the Court of Appeal, from six, four, and three months', to two months' for the principal offender, and one month each for the two other defendants, are generally considered lenient.

It has also been commented on that Mr. Blunt's letter, criticizing the Egyptian Courts for their severity towards natives in cases of this description, which appeared in all the Arab papers, should have been published while the appeal was still pending.

I have, &c.

(Signed) RENNELL RODD

NO. 23.

Viscount Cromer to the Marquess of Lansdowne.—(Received August 30.)

My Lord, Strathmore Lodge, Halkirk, August 27, 1901

I THOUGHT it desirable to send Mr. Wilfrid Blunt's letter of the 10th August to Mr. McIlwraith, the Judicial Adviser of the Egyptian Government. I have now the honour to inclose a copy of Mr. McIlwraith's reply.

In spite of the improvements of late years, no one, as Mr. McIlwraith very justly remarks, supposes that the administration of justice in Egypt is by any means perfect. I believe, however, the native Judges to be a body of very honourable men, who, on the whole, perform their duties fearlessly, and to the best of their ability. I have, equally with Mr. McIlwraith, occasionally heard suggestions of racial prejudice; but the accusation that, for whatever reason, any predisposition exists to punish offenders against Europeans, whether of British or of any other nationality, with excessive severity, is somewhat novel. Until it is supported by better testimony than any that Mr. Wilfrid Blunt has produced, I shall venture to think that it is unfounded.

Sir Rennell Rodd's despatches deal so fully with the merits of the particular case under discussion that any further comment on my part is unnecessary.

In so far that an involuntary trespass was committed on his property, Mr. Blunt has manifestly a legitimate cause for complaint. The officers concerned behaved as might have been expected of them. They at once apologized, and offered to pay for whatever trifling damage they had unwittingly caused. I do not see what more, under the circumstances, they could have done. Many landowners in Egypt would, I cannot but think, have been satisfied with these explanations. I trust, however, that the attention which Mr. Blunt has drawn to the subject, together with the instructions which I understand have been or are about to be sent by the War Office to Egypt, will insure that for the future great care will be taken that no acts of trespass are committed by the officers of the British army.

On the other hand, the fact of the trespass does not in any adequate degree justify the conduct of Mr. Blunt's employés.

They committed assaults for which they were very properly punished by the competent tribunal. I am unable to agree with Mr. Blunt's views that no prosecution should have taken place. Disputes involving litigation between the officers and soldiers of the Army of Occupation on the one hand, and Egyptians on the other hand, are fortunately of rare occurrence. When, however, the soldier is the accused party, he is tried by court-martial—a tribunal which certainly does not in any degree evince a tendency to palliate offences committed against the civil population. It is essential that when, as in the present case, the aggrieved parties are British officers or soldiers, they should be able to look with confidence to the Civil Courts to afford them adequate protection against illegality or injustice.

I have only to add that the whole incident, the gravity of which appears to me to have been much exaggerated by Mr. Blunt, is one of very trifling importance.

I have, &c.

(Signed) CROMER

INCLOSURE IN NO. 23.
Memorandum by Mr. MccIlwraith.

AS regards the merits of this particular case, and the justice or otherwise of the sentences pronounced in first instance, and on appeal, I am unable to express any opinion, as I am still awaiting an official report of the case from the Parquet in Cairo.

But as regards the statements contained in Mr. Blunt's Memorandum to Lord Lansdowne, to which you draw my attention, and which are similar in tone to those which I had already observed—with some regret—in his letter to the "Standard", I should like to say a word.

The suggestion that the Egyptian Summary Court Judges are generally under the impression that the English Adviser at the Ministry of Justice only expects them "to act honestly and fearlessly" where natives alone are concerned, is quite unwarranted by the facts; nor is the statement that they give their judgement "in fear and trembling, and almost always in the Englishman's favour", at all borne out by experience. As regards the first imputation, I have frequently been at pains to impress upon them that what we want from them is simply justice, as between man and man, irrespective of creeds and nationalities; and I believe that the bulk of the native Magistracy are now perfectly well aware that "to act honestly and fearlessly" in all cases that come before them is the surest road to official favour and promotion.

Again, the allegation that where Englishmen are concerned the native Judge "will almost always give judgement in their favour" is so far removed from the truth that, as a matter of act, I have been compelled of late, on more than one occasion, to expostulate with Judges who systematically award inadequate sentences in cases of assault on Englishmen, and to point out to them that, whilst we certainly demand no more from them for Englishmen than for natives, neither are we at all disposed to take less. I may refer notably to certain recent cases of assault on employés of the Egyptian Markets Company.

This enterprise has a considerable number of young English Inspectors in its employ, whose duty it is to visit the various cattle markets scattered about the country and report irregularities to headquarters.

There have been recently several very gross and unprovoked assault committed by fellaheen on these Inspectors where—on subsequent prosecution—the sentences awarded by the Summary Court Judges have been, I regret to say, quite derisory.

I was present in Court at the hearing of one of these cases, and I have little hesitation in saying that if the victim had been an Egyptian Effendi, instead of a comparatively unknown Englishman, the sentence would have been three months instead of eight days.

I think it is clear therefore that if the native Judges occasionally err—and nobody pretends that they are perfect yet—it is rather on the side of racial prejudice than that of terrorized servility; and one cannot help regretting that, led astray either by an imperfect acquaintance with these Courts, in their present stage of development, or by a personal bias in a case affecting his own household. Mr. Blunt should have been induced to give currency to representations concerning them which are so widely removed from the truth.

(Signed) MALCOLM McILWRAITH.
Royal Hotel, North Berwick
August 24, 1901.

NO. 24.

War Office to Foreign Office.—(Received August 29.)
Sir, War Office,   August 28, 1901

I AM directed by the Secretary of State for War to transmit to you the inclosed copy of correspondence regarding the trespass of British officers on the property of Mr. Wilfrid Blunt at Cairo and the circumstances which ensued in consequence.

2. I am to add that the case is still under the consideration of the Commander-in-Chief.

I am, &c.

(Signed) G. FLEETWOOD WILSON.

INCLOSURE 1 IN NO. 24.

General Officer Commanding in Egypt to Adjutant-General.
(Extract.)   Cairo, August 15, 1901.

I HAVE the honour to inclose a cutting from the "Standard" of the 6th instant, in which Mr. Wilfrid Blunt draws attention to the case of an assault committed by some of his employés here on certain officers at present quartered in Cairo.

Herewith I send a full report of the case for the information of the Field-Marshal Commander-in-chief.

The inclosure marked (A) is the first Report sent to me of the affair immediately after its occurrence.

The inclosure (C) is a further Report I called for from Major Rycroft, in temporary command of the 11th Hussars, after the publication of Mr. Blunt's letter.

The inclosure (B) is a letter that Major Rycroft sent to Mr. Blunt, with a copy of Report (A), to inform him of the assault.

On my receiving Report (A) I immediately put myself in communication with Sir Rennell Rodd (Acting Agent and Consul-General) and Mr. Machell (Adviser to the Minister of the Interior) and pressed strongly for the arrest of the natives who had committed the assault and for their trial as soon as possible. The matter was placed in the hands of the Parquet, which decided to prosecute.

The responsibility is mine alone for the insistence of arrest and trial. Mr. Blunt is absolutely wrong in placing this responsibility on Major Rycroft. That, however, is only one of Mr. Blunt's many misstatements.

The fact that the officers never struck, or retaliated on, the natives was chiefly, I am convinced, attributable to the commonsense and tact displayed by Major Rycroft. Being able to speak to the natives in Arabic, he was able to quiet them and prevent the assault from being of a graver nature, the consequences of which would probably have been of a most disastrous nature to the natives.

The assault was as unjustifiable as the remarks made by Mr. Blunt about a gallant English regiment are unpardonable; his annoyance can be no excuse for his many mis-statements.

Major Rycroft showed the proper gentleman-like feeling in expressing regret for the trespass, and I cannot but hope that Mr. Blunt will display the same feeling when he is in possession of the true facts of the case.

INCLOSURE 2 IN NO. 24.

Letter from Mr. Wilfrid Blunt to the "Standard", August 4, 1901.

[See No. 9.]

INCLOSURE 3 IN NO. 24.(A.)

Report from Major Rycroft to the Chief Staff officer, July 21, 1901.

[See Inclosure in No. 8.]

INCLOSURE 4 IN NO. 24. (B.)

Major Rycroft to Mr. Wilfrid Blunt.

Dear Sir, Abbassiyeh, Cairo, July 21, 1901.

I BEG to inclose copy of a Report made by me this morning giving the actual facts of an unfortunate occurrence which took place on your property today.

The greatest forbearance was shown by myself and the other officers, without which a very serious fracas must have occurred.

I am able to talk Arabic, so understood the insulting and insolent language used by the Bedouin Moutlak.

Regretting that such an incident should have occurred.

(Signed) W. H. RYCROFT, Major,
11th Hussars.

INCLOSURE 5 IN NO. 24. (C.)

Further Statement to Assault on Officers on July 21, 1901.

MR. BLUNT'S property is bordered on the desert side by a lowish wall, with a cactus hedge on the inside, and Captain Harman, with the hounds, moving towards Birket-El-Haj, was riding along a path which runs between the wall and a dry canal, and had no intention of drawing Mr. Blunt's cultivated inclosure. The hounds, evidently winding a fox, jumped the wall and went off full cry into cultivated ground.

Captain Harman and the whips galloped for the hole in the wall, and it was while going through this that they were first struck at. They then galloped across an open piece of ground and over a bank fringed with trees, and I then heard Captain Harman blow his horn, evidently with the object of withdrawing his hounds. The "field" remained outside, but hearing a lot of shouting in Arabic, I called to the other officers, and, going through the hole in the wall, galloped across an open uncultivated field and over a bank, where I found Captain Harman and the hounds, with a crowd of natives in a very excited state.

Captain Harman was surrounded by his hounds, having managed to withdraw them from the line of the fox, which they most certainly had never killed.

From the time when Captain Harman went through the hole in the wall to when I joined him was, at the outside, four minutes. I then distinctly explained in Arabic to the natives who we were, when Moutlak, pointing at Captain Harman, shouted in Arabic that he (Captain Harman) was no officer, but worse than any Soudanese syce. However, on my ordering him to hold his tongue, he stopped his abuse.

I then asked for a pencil and paper, stating that I must have their names, and would give them mine, and we moved towards the exit, Moutlak telling me that he would there give me pencil, &c. We went at a walk, and it was then that Lieutenant Sir Brodrick Hartwell, who turned back to bring on a lagging hound, was surrounded and struck from behind.

On arriving at the exit Captain Harman, with the hounds, and most of the officers went outside, but I remained just inside waiting for pencil and paper, but as these were slow of coming, and one of the natives pointing out a house where, he said, resided Mr. Blunt's Wakil (i.e., agent), I said we would all go there, and moved quietly to the opening in the wall, as the house pointed out to us was outside the inclosure, and distant about a quarter of a mile.

The officers (two or three in number) still in the inclosure, of whom Lieutenant Cayzer was one, followed, and Mohamed the Ghaffir rushed and seized my bridle, as though to prevent me going out. He, however, dropped it and I moved on. Several Arabs, however, got between me and the officers, and striking at them tried to prevent them leaving the enclosure.

Having in my previous Report stated what occurred after this, I hope that the Major-General Commanding will find this statement sufficiently clear and full.

(Signed) W. H. RYCROFT, Major,
11th Hussars

NO. 25.
Foreign Office to Mr. Wilfrid Blunt.
Sir,   Foreign Office, August 29, 1901

VISCOUNT CRANBORNE has laid before the Marquess of Lansdowne your letter of the 17th instant, relative to an answer given in the House of Commons to a question asked by Sir Charles Cayzer, M.P.

A report of the question and answer is inclosed herewith.

Sir Charles Cayzer inquired whether the Under-Secretary of State was aware that your three Bedouin servants had some time previously, by your directions, flogged two Greeks who went into your enclosure until they were insensible.

Lord Cranborne replied that His Majesty's Government had no information of the incident mentioned, but that they understood that at the trial of the men accused of assaulting the British officers, the defendants' counsel had mentioned that he had himself witnessed a case where two Italians who had trespassed on your property were bound and severely beaten in your presence.

I am to inclose a report of this statement.

You will notice that the advocate positively re-affirmed its accuracy in conversation after the trial. Lord Cranborne confined himself strictly to mentioning that the statement had been made, and gave the authority. His answer cannot be correctly described as conveying a version of his own, or, as you have most unwarrantably suggested, one revised with a particular object.

Your letter did not reach Lord Cranborne until after the prorogation of Parliament, but your contradiction of the statement will be included in the papers which it is intended to present on the subject.

I am, &c.

(Signed) T. H. SANDERSON.

INCLOSURE 1 IN NO. 25.

Extract from the "Daily News" of August 16, 1901.

THE INCIDENT NEAR CAIRO.—Sir Charles Cayzer asked the Under-Secretary of State for Foreign Affairs if he was aware that Mr. Wilfrid Blunt's Bedouin servants, three of whom were recently punished for assaulting officers of 11th Hussars, near Cairo, some time previously, by Mr. Blunt's directions, flogged two Greeks who went into his enclosure until they were insensible; and what steps, if any, were taken in this matter.

Lord Cranborne.—His Majesty's Government have no information of the incident mentioned. They understand that at the trial of the men accused of assaulting the British officers, the defendants' counsel mentioned that he had himself witnessed a case where two Italians, who had trespassed on Mr. Blunt's property, were bound and severely beaten in Mr. Blunt's presence. If the facts were as stated, it was clearly for the sufferers to complain to the authorities or take legal remedies. It is not known whether they did so.

INCLOSURE 2 IN NO. 25.

Note by Captain Hopkinson, August 11, 1901

[See Inclosure 2 in No. 17.]

NO. 26.

Sir R. Rodd to the Marquess of Lansdowne.—(Received August 30.)

My Lord,   Cairo, August 22, 1901

WITH reference to previous correspondence, concerning the assault committed on British officers by Mr. Blunt's servants, I have the honour to transmit to your Lordship herewith copy of a letter which has appeared in a local paper, the "Bourse Egyptienne".

The writer is unknown to me, but his letter is worth perusing as showing that the case under discussion, and the incident with the two Italians, referred to by the defendants' counsel at the trial, are not isolated instances of high-handed dealing on the part of Mr. Blunt's employés.

I have, &c.

(Signed) RENNELL RODD.

INCLOSURE IN NO. 26.

Newspaper Extract.
(Translation.)

M. le Directeur,

I HAVE read in your issue of the 14th instant Major Rycroft's Report and Mr. Blunt's letter concerning the fox-hunting incident.

I do not wish to discuss the sundry opinions published in the papers, nor to take part for either the English officers or Mr. Blunt's ghaffirs; but, having lived in Matarieh for many years, I made a point of also holding a little inquiry upon my own account, so as to get at the truth out of pure curiosity.

I can to-day affirm—basing my affirmation upon definite evidence which I have obtained—that the Report of Major Rycroft is sincere and that the facts occurred as he has stated. I may add that the Arabs who gave me this evidence did not in the least dissimulate their joy at the fact that the English officers had been ill-treated by Mr. Blunt's ghaffirs.

Mr. Blunt, who believes, without, however, definitely stating it, that it was the English officers who struck the first blows; Mr. Blunt, who says that no violation of his property had taken place except "upon rare occasions by Greek or native marauders, who were easily turned out", seems to be ignorant of the manner in which his property is guarded, and does not take into any account the extent of his obligation to the tolerance of the Europeans who had so often reason to complain of his faithful ghaffirs.

The few facts which I will now give you will enable you to know more of these people, and to appreciate more fully the incidents which form the subject of Major Rycroft's Report.

These "faithful ghaffirs" are not content with guarding Mr. Blunt's estates, but imagine themselves to be the proprietors of all the surrounding land. So much so, that for some time past shooting-parties have abstained from venturing near rather than expose themselves to a row. It happens, nevertheless, that, from time to time, a party, unaware of the habits of the "faithful ghaffirs", goes to shoot in the neighbourhood. It is so much the worse for them; they are promptly assaulted by a band of brutes, who not only ill-treat them, but take away their guns from them. A certain number of guns have been taken in this manner and never restored to their owners.

In the case of absolute necessity, one could understand their conduct if the shooting-parties were found upon the estates of Mr. Blunt; this is not the case at all; it is outside the limits of his property that these occurrences happen. One sportsman, Mr. T., who lives at Zeitoun, was one day attacked by three of Mr. Blunt's ghaffirs at a considerable distance from the estate, and it was only thanks to his resolution that he was able to overawe these savages, who insisted absolutely upon taking away his gun.

The following adventure is my own personal experience:-

Towards the end of February 1888, I was going from Matarieh to Birket-el-Marg to shoot duck with a friend. We followed the desert road. Arrived at a point to the east of Mr. Blunt's property, at a distance of more than 200 metres from its boundary, my friend perceived an enormous lizard and fired at it.

The lizard was not hit, and we ran after it, assisted by our two donkey-boys, in an attempt to capture it alive. Suddenly we heard cries to our left from a party of five men, armed with long sticks, who were running towards us and gesticulating like madmen, while a sixth, a little way behind, called out to them, "Take the guns away from the dogs".

Our two donkey-boys, seized with panic, mounted their steeds and, without losing a minute, galloped off, crying:

"Run! They are Mr. Blunt's ghaffirs".

We quickly came to a decision. Resolved not to have our guns forced from us, we loaded them with No. 8 shot cartridges with the firm intention of firing at the legs of our opponents.

When they got to a point about 40 metres distant I called out to them, "Stop, or we shall fire!" and, suiting the action to the word, took aim at them. The effect was immediate. Our assailants stopped and contended themselves with calling out that "Mr. Blunt did not wish, and would not allow, a gun to be fired on his land".

I replied that we were far from Mr. Blunt's property, in the desert where Mr. Blunt had no territorial rights, and advised them to retire quickly unless they would learn to their cost how men like themselves should be treated.

The "braves" consulted among themselves, and, without heeding the exhortations of their sixth companion, who continued to call out to them to take our guns, they turned their backs on us and retired.

And this is how two peaceable sportsmen, if they had not possessed a little energy, would have suffered ill-treatment and have lost their guns, or have been under the disagreeable necessity of firing upon their assailants; and one can imagine what regrettable consequences might have resulted from this incident.

Mr. Blunt would do well, since he has arrived at the possibility of keeping tame foxes, to busy himself equally with the taming of his faithful servants a little. It would be prudent on his part.

Yours, &c.

(Signed) ARBAGUES DE SOSTEN

NO. 27.

Sir R. Rodd to the Marquess of Lansdowne.—(Received September 2.)

My Lord,   Cairo, August 25, 1901

IN accordance with your Lordship's instructions I have the honour to offer the following observations on the letter addressed to your Lordship by Mr. Wilfrid Blunt under date of the 10th instant.

In the first place I venture to submit to your Lordship, in view of the phrase employed by Mr. Blunt, "Later . . . another complexion appears to have been put on the affair", that my reports on the case have, from the first telegram despatched on the 23rd July, been entirely consistent in their exposition of the facts, to which, after due investigation, I firmly adhere.

My information was derived, in the first place, from Captain Harman himself, within a few hours of the occurrence. At the time he narrated the circumstances he was not aware that the matter would come before me officially, and his version of the story, given at lunch on the same day to myself, Mr. Baird, and Colonel Bainbridge, may be looked upon as wholly unprejudiced. As he is now in England I have not been able to see him again since the receipt of Mr. Blunt's letter. Secondly, from personal interviews with Major Rycroft, whom I have interrogated repeatedly on the question from every point of view. Thirdly, from an examination of Lieutenant Rome, the officer who first entered the enclosure with Captain Harman. And fourthly, from a consultation of the records of the Court, and conversation with the Prucureur-Général, Mohamed Safouat Bey, who conducted the prosecution.

Mr. Blunt begins by stating that it is evident, from Major Rycroft's Report, that the entrance to his property could not have been due, as reported to me, to the accident of a fox having taken refuge within his walled inclosure, but was deliberate, and proceeds to give his reasons for adopting this conclusion.

I beg to point out that I did not make the above assertion. My words in the original telegraphic Report were, "the hounds, following a scent, crossed his boundary wall".

On the morning in question, the officers, starting before daybreak from Abassiyeh with their six couple of hounds, had been drawing for foxes all along the edge of the desert. The reason of the early start made was that the foxes and jackals, which have their earths in the desert, come in at night to the cultivated grounds. At the first streak of dawn they break away for the desert. In the damp of the early morning the scent lies well, and it is thus possible to obtain a run across the desert. A very short time after the sun has risen no trace of scent remains. It was never contemplated, nor would it be possible, to ride through cotton plantations and irrigated land.

In the process of drawing for foxes, the company arrived at about 5 A.M. at the wall inclosing Mr. Blunt's property. Parenthetically it may be mentioned that the sense of the word garden, is somewhat misleading. In the part of the inclosure where the occurrence took place there are palm trees, orange and lemon trees, and considerable areas planted with cotton and beans.

I would now draw attention to the sketch map furnished by Mr. Blunt, which I return herewith for purposes of reference. The large area outside Mr.

Blunt's inclosed property, surrounded by a red line marked "open boundary of estate", has, I am told, at the present dry season of the year, when there is no water in the irrigation canal, nothing to distinguish it, when approached from Abassiyeh, from the rest of the surrounding desert, unless it may be some faint traces of old ridging for cultivation. It is possible that, when the water comes down, its aspect changes, and in the remoter parts near the wells it is possible there may actually be cultivation. There are also, doubtless, corner stones to mark Mr. Blunt's boundaries, but I am assured that there is nothing at the present time apparent to make a rider believe that he is passing over anything but desert ground. It is true that there is a notice board at some distance from the wall, of the kind used in Egypt to indicate that shooting is reserved there—in fact, the literal translation of the Arabic in the notice is to the effect that it is forbidden to shoot. I dwell upon this point because Mr. Blunt maintains that, in riding along his wall, the officers had already committed a trespass. (Footnote: Mr. Hohler, 2nd Secretary to His Majesty's Agency, has been good enough to ride over the ground in question, and confirms the above description.)

There is, moreover, between the dry irrigation canal, marked in green, and the wall of Mr. Blunt's inclosure, a path, which is not indicated on the map, and which has all the appearance of being a thoroughfare, passing the door marked "C". It was along this path that captain Harman was riding. The six couple of hounds were following. About the point marked with one red cross in the map, there are some small holes in the wall, which is in several places dilapidated. It is probable that a fox had recently passed through one of these holes making for the desert, for here the hounds struck the line of scent, or at any rate winded a fox, and jumped the wall, the scent probably lying stronger towards the vegetation than on the barren ground outside. No fox was actually found. This is what Mr. Blunt describes as "to encourage or allow hounds to leap the enclosing fence". Captain Harman, realizing what had occurred, rode hastily back to the gate marked "C", with the object of withdrawing the hounds. He found it closed, but a short distance beyond there was a gap in the wall some 12 feet wide or more, through which he entered, followed by Lieutenant Rome and Private Bradley, who were acting as whips, and was at once, according to Lieutenant Rome's statement, opposed and struck at by Moutlak. Lieutenant Rome went to try and head off the hounds, and was thus temporarily separated from Captain Harman, but heard him blowing his horn, to call the hounds off. The rest of the officers remained outside, some 50 or 70 yards off, and did not enter until attracted by the noise of a conflict.

Mr. Blunt goes on to say that, if native testimony is to count for anything, they hunted and killed a fox and a jackal in the garden before their sport could be stopped. This Mr. Blunt appears to have learned in a letter from a certain Suleiman Effendi, with which I shall deal presently. In reply to this, I would point out that, by the time Major Rycroft rejoined Captain Harman, less than five minutes after the latter had entered, the hounds were round his horse and under complete control; there was no sign or trace of their having been blooded, and I think all who are familiar with hounds will agree that it would be impossible for a fox to have been killed without those in charge of the hounds having perceived it. All the members of the hunt I have interrogated are unanimous in agreeing that no kill took place, and I cannot but think that the ingenuity of Suleiman Effendi, who reported the circumstance to Mr. Blunt by letter, has rather overreached itself, for, though not present himself, he even specified the sex of the jackal.

I trust that this further exposition of the circumstances will finally dispose of the contention that there was a deliberate intention to put in the hounds and hunt in Mr. Blunt's garden, and will conclude this portion of my argument by quoting the Judgement of the Court, which laid down: "Il est entendu que l'entrée des officiers dans la propriété de M. Blunt n'était pas volontaire, mais elle était forcée pour reprendre les chiens, et les empêcher de faire du mal, ainsi que les prévenus le savent (It is understood that the entry of the officers on Mr. Blunt's property was not of their own wish, but was necessitated in order to get the hounds back, and prevent their doing damage, as the accused are aware)".

I have asked Major Rycroft why he used the words in his Report, which, as Mr. Blunt argues, show that the intention was deliberate, and which he considers inconsistent with the exposition I have given, viz., "the hounds jumped the low wall and immediately got on the line of a fox". Major Rycroft admits that the wording is misleading; he meant, and intended to say, "the hounds got on the line of a fox, and immediately jumped the low wall". Not realizing the importance which was to be given to this matter and to his statement, he had not weighed his words as carefully as he might have done.

I trust that I have now shown that there are no grounds for Mr. Blunt's assertion that, when the case was brought before Mr. Machell, the English adviser, "another complexion" was put upon the affair. Mr. Machell in a matter of this kind merely acts as a channel of communication, and on learning from the General Officer Commanding in Egypt what had occurred, sent the case on to the Parquet, whose business it is, in such matters, to conduct a preliminary investigation and see whether a case lies for prosecution.

With regard to the special points to which attention is drawn in numbered paragraphs, I have to observe:-

(1.) The use of the word "stones" is apparently incorrect; the missiles thrown were clods of earth, which when baked in the sun are very hard. For controversial purposes there may be a distinction , but materially the difference is slight.

(2.) With regard to the damage done, I cannot do better than transmit to your Lordship a translation of the "Procès-verbal de Constatation", drawn up by the

Parquet after careful examination of the premises, which entirely corroborates Major Rycroft's statement, and shows that the damage done was practically nil. Suleiman Effendi, Mr. Blunt's tenant, whose letter he quotes, and who made the categorical charges against the officers of acts of aggression, as well as of having killed a fox and a she-jackal, was, as is proved by the preliminary investigation conducted by the police and Parquet, not there at all, but absent in his village, while two or three of his workmen who were examined by the police deposed that they saw nothing. His evidence may therefore be dismissed.

(3.) Blows struck by the officers. I have gone into this matter very carefully, and cannot agree with Mr. Blunt that there is any reason for doubting the word and evidence of honourable gentlemen. It appears that there were only two whips among the party, the rest carrying only light riding canes, while Lieutenant Rome, one of the first to enter, had nothing at all in his hand. The only instance I can find of a blow being struck was one in self-defence at the very end of the episode, when, as the party was riding out, a man running after Lieutenant Hartwell, who was rounding off a straying hound, struck him violently on the back; he then struck out behind him in self-defence with his whip, and, it is probable, reached his assailant. One of the men accused, in fact, deposed that the lash of a whip curled round his wrist, but the medical examination at the preliminary inquiry went to show that it was doubtful whether a mark which he exhibited could be due to the lash of a whip taking effect in the manner described. With this isolated exception, which was, under the circumstances, quite justifiable, every one seems to have refrained, under Major Rycroft's control, from retaliation. It became, as Captain Harman at the time explained to me, difficult to manage the horses, which were struck repeatedly, and this added an element of danger to the situation.

(4.) The question of the blows struck by Mr. Blunt's men is dealt with in evidence before the Court, and I do not think it necessary for me to take any notice of the insinuation that British officers were "more frightened than hurt". With regard to Hamouda Effendi, Mr. Blunt points out that I am in error in describing him as his steward. He was alluded to my Moutlak as the "Wakyl", a word which may be rendered manager or steward; or it may also be interpreted as a person who takes charge in the absence of the proprietor. I rendered it in the former sense, understanding that Moutlak had described him as the "Wakyl". The point, however, is immaterial. Hamouda Effendi was in bed at the time of the occurrence, but, when the party proceeded to his house, he got up and behaved very courteously, identifying the aggressors, who had hitherto, when asked for their names, merely stated that they were all of them "Blunt". Hamouda Effendi, however, did not witness the occurrence, and his evidence is therefore only hearsay. Major Rycroft denies that he called upon him to apologize on behalf of the servants, but says that, at the preliminary inquiry, he asked him to withdraw the case.

(5.) I do not think this paragraph calls for any observations on my part, but with reference to the concluding words, "He was only obeying my orders in using the force necessary to eject the intruders", it has already been pointed out to your Lordship that the present appears not be by any means an isolated case of violence on the part of Mr. Blunt's watchmen and servants.

In conclusion, I have only to say that I do not see any justification for modifying the conclusions I have previously reported to your Lordship, by the light of the various hypotheses which Mr. Blunt has put forward, and I trust that he will no longer see any reason to doubt the word and good faith of a number of English gentlemen, who, I am sure, regret, as much as he does, the unfortunate circumstances which have brought them into conflict with him.

I now pass to a more serious consideration, namely, the aspersions which are cast in Mr. Blunt's letter on the impartiality of the judicial bench in Egypt in dealing with cases between Englishmen and natives.

It is somewhat difficult to deal with charges which are general and vague in character, and unsupported by any concrete instances, but their assertion does not imply their truth, and I may be pardoned for questioning whether, upon such a subject, Mr. Blunt can be held to speak with authority.

In the first place, with regard to what he describes as the "Cadis or County Court Judges" (the name "Cadi" is now usually applied in English only to the

Judges who interpret the Sherin, or religious law, and it would be more correct to describe the class to which Mr. Blunt refers as "Judges of the Courts of First Instance"), it is stated that they owe all chances of promotion to the good will of the English Adviser of the Ministry of Justice, and indirectly to the British Agency, as supreme authority; that, therefore, in cases between a native and an Englishman, the balance of justice in their minds is necessarily disturbed, and judgement is given, in fear and trembling, "almost always" in the Englishman's favour. Such an ex parte statement will be taken for what it is worth. It may, perhaps, be pertinent first to point out what is the position of the Judges in this category, and how their promotions are made.

The Judges of First Instance, some of the most capable of whom are told off to the Summary Courts, are, with a few exceptions, dating from the early days of the Tribunals, gentlemen who have obtained legal diplomas either at the Khedival School of Law or at one of the Law Schools in Europe. They belong to a regular service, and are divided into five categories, with different scales of salary. Promotions from one category to another are made by Khedival decree on the recommendation of the Minister of Justice, and are partly by seniority and partly according to capacity. Of capacity the English Judicial Adviser is no doubt the principal Judge, but he is necessarily guided by the professional opinion of the Presidents of the Tribunals, under whose superintendence the Judges work; of the President and Vice-President of the

Court of Appeal, before whom appeals from their decisions come; and of the Procureur-Général, who superintends all criminal prosecutions before them. It is not the practice for the British Agency to be consulted as to such promotions.

The Judges have to apply a very comprehensive and definite code. Their latitude and discretion lie in the appreciation of evidence and the limitation of punishments. There is no doubt that the Tribunals would attach considerable importance to the evidence of Englishmen, not least to that of officers of senior rank. That their evidence would weigh, perhaps, somewhat preponderatingly against the evidence of a native servant, in case of a conflict, is not, perhaps, matter for surprise in a country where perjury is, unfortunately, common, and where false witnesses can always be found to come forward.

The Judges are under the oath of their appointment to judge justly, and, so far as the experience goes of the legal authorities whim I have consulted, they cannot call to mind evidence of cases where that oath has been violated in order to curry favour with the superior authority. Cases in which Englishmen are complainants in the native Courts are not very numerous, and the decisions in such cases as there have been do not appear, as I shall show hereafter, to lend any support to Mr. Blunt's view. Except in the Summary Courts, moreover, the judgement is always that of three Judges at least, so that the individual Judge would incur no great personal responsibility for a judgement which he might suppose to be distasteful to his superiors. The presence of the British Adviser at the Ministry of Justice would, in fact, have a contrary influence to that which Mr. Blunt implies, for a judgement improperly given in favour of an Englishman, from fear of displeasing the superior authority, would undoubtedly be severely handled in the Appeal Court, and could hardly fail to come to the knowledge of the Judicial Adviser, whose impartiality in such cases Mr. Blunt will not call in question. Were such a case, therefore, to occur, it would very soon be made plain that the course was not calculated to secure promotion, and no uncertainty would be left on the mind of the Judge that, as in the cases between native and native, where Mr. Blunt admits he judges fearlessly, he will only be approved where he judges impartially in cases between natives and Englishmen also.

So much for the Judges of First Instance. I now come to the Judges in the Court of Appeal, the superiority of which Mr. Blunt admits, though he is not able to persuade himself that, in the case in which he is interested, the matter will not have been prejudged before it was brought into Court. I regret that Mr. Blunt should have expressed such an opinion to your Lordship. It will, if it becomes known here, produce a very painful impression among the honourable and eminent Egyptian gentlemen who occupy that Bench, for I take it for granted, from the nature of his arguments, that Mr. Blunt does not include in his criticisms the European Judges who sit with their Egyptian colleagues. It will, I think, be sufficient

answer to this charge to inform your Lordship that
the Judges in the Native Court of Appeal not only
receive fixed salaries, but are irremovable, and, therefore, beyond the reach of those influences to which
Mr. Blunt suggests they are amenable.

It is well, however, in answering charges of this
description, no less than in making them, to support
a general statement with some concrete evidence. It
has not been possible, in the brief time at my disposal,
to obtain comprehensive statistics of the results of
cases between British subjects and natives over a
number of years. I think, however, that sufficient justification for the views which I have submitted to
your Lordship will be afforded by a perusal of the
accompanying list of charges brought by British subjects against natives which have come under the
cognizance of the judicial authorities in Cairo during
the year 1900. (Cases in which a British subject is
prosecuted by a native go, of course, to the British
Consular Court.) I have the honour to inclose at the
same time an explanatory note, briefly analyzing the
cases on this list, which has been furnished to me by
the Acting Procureur-Général. Your Lordship will
perceive that, in all, seventy-two cases were brought
to the knowledge of the authorities. In twenty-nine
of these cases the Parquet took no action. Of these
twenty-nine charges, however, eight were against persons unknown, and may therefore be eliminated. This
leaves twenty-one cases in which the Parquet, on various grounds, decided not to prosecute. One case
only, No. 68, was brought before the criminal

Tribunal, and thirty-six charges were dealt with by the "Tribunal des Contraventions" and the "Tribunal Correctionnel". In six of these cases the accused were acquitted, those recorded under Nos. 27 and 56 being worthy of special attention.

The average number of acquittals in misdemeanour cases, where both parties are natives, is about 9 per cent. The average number of acquittals in the list of cases now submitted, where the Parquet prosecuted on behalf of a British subject, is nearly 16 per cent.

The nature of the sentences varies, of course, according to the gravity of the cases, from fines of 1s. to considerable terms of imprisonment; and it is noticeable that in one instance, No. 51, a small fine imposed by the Court of First Instance was commuted into a month's imprisonment by the Court of Appeal.

So much for the contention that Judgement is given "in fear and trembling, and always in the Englishman's favour". As an instance of the spirit which animates the judicial authorities in Egypt, I may also point out that the very case under consideration would, in the ordinary course of justice, have gone on appeal from the Summary Court to the Court of First Instance. If the appeal is made, however, by the Procureur-Général, he is able, under certain conditions, to obtain the hearing in the Court of Appeal itself. Safouat Bey, most wisely, took this course, and, by lodging a formal appeal, referred the final decision to the highest judicial authority available.

With regard to the procedure which, Mr. Blunt conjectures, must have taken place before the case could have been brought into Court:-

(a.) They must have obtained the approval of the English General in command at Cairo. Yes; the General officer in command referred the case to the Interior.

(b.) Of the English Adviser to the Ministry of the Interior. The approval of the Adviser is not necessary; he would only act as a channel of communication, placing the complaint in the hands of the Parquet.

(c.) Of the English Adviser of the Ministry of Justice. He is and was at the time absent in England on leave, and during his absence no one replaces him.

(d.) Of the British Agency. I was informed by the General that he had referred the case to the Interior, and by the Adviser to the Interior that he had sent the case on to the Parquet for investigation; but I was not consulted beforehand. Once the matter was in the hands of the Parquet it would not have been proper for me to intervene, even if I had seen reason to do so, which I certainly did not. I mention this point, not with a view to deprecating responsibility, which in approving the General's action I most readily assume, but simply to establish the point of fact. The utmost length I could have gone would have been to ask the General to withdraw the charge. However desirous I might be, in view of personal relations with Mr. Blunt, to spare him a painful incident, such an attitude on my part would, I submit, have been extremely reprehensible.

Mr. Blunt considers that the case should "never have been brought before the Courts, least of all before the native Courts". With the first part of this expression of opinion I venture to disagree; with regard to the second, I have only to state that the native Courts were the only Courts which could take cognizance of it.

There is, indeed, a special Court, with very far-reaching powers, from whose sentences there is no appeal, which may be convened, in exceptional circumstances, to try offences against officers and men of the army of occupation. This Court has only been assembled twice, to my knowledge, since it was instituted, and in both cases for offences of a very grave character against soldiers in uniform in the execution of their duty. It would have been entirely contrary to the spirit and intention in which that Tribunal was constituted to convene it in order to try an affair of this nature, which, though characterized by Mr. Blunt as one "of such great public scandal", had attracted no attention in Egypt until Mr. Blunt's communications to the press had reached this country. With regard to those communications, I cannot but think it was regrettable that Mr. Blunt should have criticized the impartiality of the Egyptian Bench while the case was still before the Court of Appeal, and should have publicly announced, on such evidence as he then possessed, that in England such a case would have been dismissed without hesitation. These utterances have, indeed, attracted some attention here.

The sentences passed in the Summary Court

were, as I had the honour to express to your Lordship, in my opinion somewhat severe; the sentences as revised on appeal are perhaps somewhat light; the difference between them marks the independence of the bench, and I have no fear that the reputation of either English or Egyptian justice will suffer from the publicity which has been given to this matter.

I have, &c.

(Signed) RENNELL RODD.

INCLOSURE 1 IN NO. 27.

Procès-verbal de Constatation.
(Translation.)

WE went to the spot to inspect it de visu, and we found on the road on the edge of the Gabaloineh Canal a notice-board, on which was written, "It is forbidden to use fire-arms", in three languages, Arabic, French, and English. This canal is a few metres distant from the wall of Mr. Blunt's property. This property, which, according to the statement of Hamoudah Effendi Abdou, the lawyer, is about 200 feddans (1 feddan = 1.038 acres) in extent, is surrounded by a wall built of mud, which is in bad repair.

The accused, Moutlak, who was with us, led us to a large gap in the said wall, through which the horses had entered. This gap is about 8 metres broad, and is open down to the level of the ground. On entering, we found an empty and uncultivated space; we walked for ten or fifteen minutes until we arrived at a second wall, which is very low. On passing through it, by means of a gap in it, we found a field, of which a very small part (approximately ½ feddan) was laid down in loubia (haricot beans), the remainder being planted with cotton. The accused, Moutlak, showed us, and we verified it, that some plants, but very few, were bent but not destroyed, and it was impossible to say whether that was the result of the trampling of horses or of men, or from any other cause, because the plants were very little bent.

Moutlak showed us, and we verified it, that there were holes near the cotton plants, which we were informed was the result of horses' hoofs, but there is nothing to prove clearly whether the holes are due to that or any other cause. The examination showed us that no damage has been done to the cotton. As for the haricot beans, five or six plants had been trampled on.

On this examination, the present procès-verbal has been drawn up and signed.

The Clerk,
(Signed) ABDEL LATIF.
The Chef de Parquet,
ABDUL MEGHID RADOUAN.

We found Mr. Blunt's horses to the right of the gap in the first wall. Moutlak told us that this spot was kept apart for the horses.

(Same signatures.)

NO. 28.

*Mr. Wilfrid Blunt to the Marquess of Lansdowne.—
(Received September 2.)*

My Lord, Newbuildings Place, Horsham, August 31,
1901

I OWE your Lordship and apology for having used
words in my letter to Lord Cranborne which have
seemed to imply that Sir Charles Cayzer's story was
"revised" at the Foreign Office. Nothing was farther
from my thought. Knowing as well as I do the traditions of the Office, I was fully aware that Lord
Cranborne's answer must have been drafted on information, however erroneous, of an official kind. What
seemed to me less consonant with tradition and courteous usage was that the answer should have been
drafted and made in the House of Commons without
previous reference to me, although I was at the time
in close communication with the Office, and a word
from me would have informed your Lordship and
Lord Cranborne that the tale was untrue.

With regard to Captain Hopkinson's Report, it is
clearly based on error. Either Hamouda Effendi was
carried away by his forensic zeal beyond what his
knowledge justified, or, what is more probable,
Captain Hopkinson misunderstood his words and
unconsciously denaturalized them in translation.
Nothing in the condensed Arabic report of the trial
sent me resolves this doubt. I would point out, however, to your Lordship that, even accepting Captain
Hopkinson's Report as accurate, the words of Lord

Cranborne's answer do not exactly correspond with it. Captain Hopkinson's words are not "bound and severely beaten in Mr. Blunt's presence", but "Mr. Blunt was present, and asked, &c", leaving it in doubt whether the speaker quoted (and he was pleading in Arabic) meant present at the alleged flogging or merely present in the sense of not being absent from home. I do not quite understand why the text should have been thus altered, unless it was due to a telegraphic variation your Lordship may have received of it from Cairo. It will be remembered that just such a variation changed the sense of Major Rycroft's Report, to the extent that it was at first believed at the Foreign Office that the officers followed a fox into my inclosure, and not, as the Report, when it arrived, proved, found one inside. I feel sure that neither your Lordship nor Lord Cranborne would have knowingly accentuated the tale in my disfavour.

Be this, however, as it may, and whatever may have been said by Hamouda Effendi, or understood by Captain Hopkinson at the trial, the tale itself is a mistake and a calumny. At no time has any person, European or native, been, as suggested, bound and flogged in my garden, either in my presence or, I am almost equally certain, in my absence. With the exception of the single exceptional instance mentioned in my letter to Lord Cranborne, the force used by me and my servants against armed trespassers has been no more than was necessary to convince them that their discharging of fire-arms would not be tolerated. It has been the menace of blows rather than blows actually delivered. But it is not always easy for native guardians, nor has it been for myself, to make such armed European intruders understand that we are in earnest with them without the application of more than words. Whether it is legal or illegal for a native Egyptian to interfere with or use force to a European trespassing with fire-arms on his land or in his garden I do not know, but I know that the law provides him with no legal remedy. I will cite an instance, which will show your Lordship how the case stands.

A few years ago, a Greek of bad repute came and established himself outside the village nearest me and set up a drinking shop, in spite of a Petition against it signed by the inhabitants, who were all Mahommedans. This Greek, with his companions, being Europeans, were allowed to carry fire-arms, the natives being forbidden, and so terrorized the district, entering where they would, on lands and in gardens. In a single year, with his shot-gun, he wounded a child, a girl of 4 years old, sitting in her father's palm garden; he wounded a local guardian of the peace, and he intentionally shot a peasant, with whom he had a dispute about water. The last-named wounded man was in hospital for several weeks, and twenty-two shots were extracted from him. Yet it was found impossible to bring the man in any way to justice. Having paid the hospital dues with which the wounded peasant was charged, I laid the case before our English authorities, and saw the then Native Minister. All were most anxious to help, but could suggest no remedy, though it was hinted to me that one lay in the peasants' own hands if they had the courage. This was several years ago; but things are still hardly better. Only last autumn I consulted Mr. Machell on the whole question of European vagabondage, and asked his advice how to act; but, beyond showing me a draft of proposed Regulations, most of which he had not been able to get accepted, he was as unable as the others had been to say what could be done. The truth is that there is no protection for the fellaheen, or, indeed, for any one living in the country districts of Egypt, except such force or intim- idation or persuasion as he can exercise against European marauders.

I trust that your Lordship will accept this renewed denial by me of Sir Charles Cayzer's story and all its variants as final and sufficient, and that, the Session being now over, my present letter, with my letter to Lord Cranborne and the rest of my corre- spondence with the Foreign Office, may be included in the papers promised to be laid before Parliament.

I have, &c.

(Signed) WILFRID SCAWEN BLUNT

NO. 29.

Foreign Office to War Office.

Sir,   Foreign Office, September 4, 1901

WITH reference to my letter of the 29th ultimo for- warding correspondence respecting the assault committed upon some British officers by native servants on Mr. Blunt's property near Cairo, I am directed by the Marquess of Lansdowne to transmit, for the information of the Secretary of State for War, copy of a despatch from the Earl of Cromer, inclosing a Memorandum by the Judicial Adviser of the Egyptian Government (No. 23.), and giving his own views on the incident. I am also to inclose copy of a despatch from Sir R. Rodd (No. 27.), His Majesty's Acting Agent and Consul-General in Egypt, answering in detail the statements made in Mr. Blunt's letter to Lord Lansdowne of the 10th ultimo.

Lord Lansdowne entirely concurs in the opinions expressed by Lord Cromer and by Sir R. Rodd in these and in previous despatches from the latter officers, of which copies were forwarded to you in my previous letter. It is impossible, in his Lordship's opinion, to attach serious weight to the charges brought by Mr. Blunt against the officers concerned. These charges appear to be founded largely on conjecture, supported by ingenious attempts to pervert or discover flaws in Major Rycroft's perfectly straightforward report, which has been confirmed by the sworn evidence given at the trial.

Lord Lansdowne considers that credit is due to Major Rycroft for the self-control which he exercised and induced his brother officers to show under circumstances of great provocation. It is to be regretted that a trespass should have been committed on Mr. Blunt's property, though an involuntary one. Mr. Blunt has been offered all the reparation that is possible under the circumstances, but Lord Lansdowne thinks that Mr. Secretary Brodrick will agree that all possible care should be taken to avoid acts of trespass by British officers on inclosed or cultivated property, and he would suggest that instructions to that effect should be sent to the General Officer Commanding in Egypt.

I am to inclose a draft of a letter which, with Mr. Brodrick's concurrence, Lord Lansdowne would propose to address to Mr. Blunt, inclosing an extract of Major-General Lane's report (No. 33.)

I am, &c.

(Signed) T. H. SANDERSON

NO. 30.

Foreign Office to Mr. Wilfrid Blunt.

Sir,   Foreign Office, September 9, 1901

I AM directed by the Marquess of Lansdowne to acknowledge the receipt of your letter of the 31st ultimo relative to the report that two Italians who had trespassed on your property near Cairo had been tied up and beaten by your servants.

I am to inform you that your letter will, in accordance with your request, in included in the papers to be laid before Parliament in connection with the assault made by your servants on British officers.

I am, &c.

(Signed) T. H. SANDERSON.

NO. 31.

Sir R. Rodd to the Marquess of Lansdowne.—(Received September 9.)

My Lord,   Cairo, August 30, 1901

I HAVE the honour to acknowledge the receipt of your Lordship's despatch of the 23rd instant, inclosing a letter from Mr. Blunt, in which he denies the truth of the statement reported to have been made at the trial of his servants, by the advocate for the defence, to the effect that he had seen two Italians bound and beaten in Mr. Blunt's presence.

Whether or not this story has grown out of the incident referred to in Mr. Blunt's letter is, I venture to submit, rather a question for him to discuss with Hamouda Bey, whose statement was reported to me by the Inspector of the Ministry of the Interior, present at the trial. But that evidence of violence on the part of his watchmen is not wanting is, I think, not only apparent from the letter to the local press, which was forwarded to your Lordship in my despatch of the 22nd instant, but is also corroborated by a further letter, copy of which I have the honour to inclose, which appeared shortly afterwards in the "Egyptian Gazette".

I also inclose, for your Lordship's information, an extract from a letter to the Adviser to the Interior, written by a prominent French official in the Egyptian Government service, who would not, however, wish his name to appear in this correspondence.

With regard to the concluding observations in

Mr. Blunt's letter, I should be sorry to suggest that the police organization in this country is by any means perfect. At the same time, in view of the fact that Mr. Blunt's property is situated on a railway line, some 200 yards from the station, and only a few miles out of Cairo, it would seem to lie rather in the category of suburban than of country districts; and seeing that there is a police station about a mile away at Marg, the further end of the suburban line, and a coastguard station not five minutes walk from his stables, I remain unconvinced that there is any necessity for the owner to proclaim martial law on his property, or to take its execution into his own hands.

I have, &c.

(Signed) RENNELL RODD.

INCLOSURE 1 IN NO. 31.
Extract from the "Egyptian Gazette" of August 26, 1901.

SPORT AT MATARIEH.

To the Editor of the "Egyptian Gazette".

Sir,

IN supporting M. Arbagues de Sosten's statement in to-day's "Gazette", may I furnish an instance of what happened to a friend of mine? I cannot say anything about the boundary, but my friend, as in the case of the lizard, had a wounded duck to get, and in doing so was surrounded and very roughly knocked about in fighting for his gun. His servant too, who came to his assistance, received a very severe mauling. They were eventually overpowered and led off prisoners to Mr. Blunt's house. After keeping them waiting for over an hour, Mr. Blunt came down in Arab dress, heard the case on both sides, and, in passing judgement, after the manner of a Judge dealing with a first offender, informed my friend what would happen if he came before him again. My friend then asked who his interrogator was, and the latter replied, "I am Mr. Blunt". Then my friend asked for his gun. "Oh!" was the reply he got; "you have lost that;" and after some further irrelevant remarks, Mr. Blunt continued, "Well, this time you may have it back, but if it happens again you will not get it returned". My friend was then escorted off the place.

I am, &c.

(Signed) A SPORTSMAN.

INCLOSURE 2 IN NO. 31.

Extract from a Letter to the Adviser to the Ministry of the Interior.

(Translation.)

SOME seven or eight years ago, while out shooting on the ground next Mr. Blunt's property, and which has since been bought by him, I had just shot two doves, when the gaffirs of the property came out through a breach in the wall and advanced towards me with raised sticks and abusive language.

Fortunately, I kept cool and drew their attention to the fact that I was not within the property. They continued to threaten me. I was accompanied by my shikari, a young Bedouin, who is devoted to me, and who tried to calm the gaffirs. In any case, I do not know how the affair would have terminated, for I had my gun loaded, without the intervention of a European jockey, Kennedy, who was then in the service of Mr. Blunt, and who came up a few minutes afterwards. He calmed the gaffirs, and gave me to understand that they had the most stringent orders.

NO. 32.

War Office to Foreign Office.—(Received September 11.)
Sir,   War Office, September 10, 1901

I AM directed by the Secretary of State for War to acknowledge the receipt of your letters of the 29th ultimo and the 4th and 7th instant, forwarding correspondence in regard to the assault committed upon some British officers by native servants on Mr. W. Blunt's property near Cairo.

2. In reply, I am to acquaint you, for the information of the Marquess of Lansdowne, that Mr. Secretary Brodrick concurs with the draft of the letter his Lordship proposes to address to Mr. Blunt.

3. A communication on this subject is being addressed to the General officer Commanding the Forces in Egypt, requesting that he will issue instructions directing that all possible care should be taken to avoid acts of trespass by British officers on inclosed or cultivated property.

4. It has also been intimated that the Commander-in-chief will be glad if hunting on Sundays is discontinued.

I am, &c.

(Signed) G. FLEETWOOD WILSON.

NO. 33.

Foreign Office to Mr. Wilfrid Blunt.

Sir,   Foreign Office, September 11, 1901

I AM directed by the marquess of Lansdowne to state that your letter of the 10th ultimo relative to the assault committed by servants on your property near Cairo on a party of British officers was forwarded to His Majesty's Acting Agent and Consul-General at Cairo, and I am to transmit to you copy of a despatch from Sir R. Rodd, containing his observations (No. 17).

Sir R. Rodd had in the meanwhile addressed a despatch to Lord Lansdowne, forwarding a report of the proceedings at the trial of your servants, and commenting on the statements made in a letter previously written by you to the editor of the "Standard".

I am to transmit to you a copy of this despatch and its inclosures (No. 27), together with an extract of a report from Major-General Lane (Inclosure 1 in No. 24), the General in Command of the troops in Egypt, which has been communicated by the Secretary of State for War.

It appears from these papers that the account of the incident given in your letters to the "Standard" and to Lord Lansdowne must have been written under a misapprehension of the facts. It is clear that your statements, and the comments which you have founded upon them, are not justified by what actually occurred.

Major-General Lane states that the responsibility for applying for the arrest and trial of your servants rests with him, not with Major Rycroft.

Lord Lansdowne considers that Major-General Lane was right in thus acting, and that the decision of the Egyptian legal authorities to prosecute the offenders was correct. The sentences imposed by the Summary Court may have been somewhat severe, but as subsequently modified by the Court of Appeal they do not appear to Lord Lansdowne to be otherwise than just and proportionate to the offence committed. It would be altogether contrary to the practice of His Majesty's Government to interfere in such a matter unless there were evidence of some palpable injustice. In the present case, Lord Lansdowne sees no reason for such interference.

The incident is to be regretted, but it is largely due to the instructions which you gave to your servants and to the interpretation which they placed upon them. Lord Lansdowne cannot but think it culpable to have left with them orders which could be so interpreted, and for any scandal which may have resulted he considers that you must be held mainly responsible. It was owing only to the self-control exercised by Major Rycroft and the other officers, under circumstances of great provocation, that the affair did not assume a much more serious character. The trespass committed on your garden was involuntary, and as the officers concerned have offered their apologies and compensation for any damage that may have been committed, and such damage is shown on investigation to have been insignificant, Lord Lansdowne does not consider that you have reasonable ground for further complaint on this score. But he has suggested to the Secretary of State for War that instructions should be sent to the General Commanding in Egypt that all possible care should in future be taken to avoid acts of trespass by British officers on inclosed or cultivated property. He has been informed by Mr. Brodrick that instructions to this effect will be issued.

I am, &c.

(Signed) T. H. SANDERSON.

NO. 34.

Sir R. Rodd to the Marquess of Lansdowne.—(Received September 13.)

(Telegraphic.)   Cairo, September 13, 1901

WITH reference to the letter from Mr. Blunt to Lord Lansdowne of the 31st August, of which I have received copy, I have to state that the interpreter of the Army of Occupation, who was present at the trial, confirms Captain Hopkinson's statement which forms Inclosure 2 in my despatch of the 12th August. The statement was checked by Captain Hopkinson's interpreter, and Captain Hopkinson himself adheres to it as correctly conveying the impression produced by the words of Counsel, who used argument that Mr. Blunt was cognizant of what occurred in order to prove non-responsibility on the part of his servants.

In stating that Mr. Blunt asked him what he should do with the Italians, Hamouda Effendi certainly gave the Court the impression that Mr. Blunt was cognizant of the affair. As regards the actual punishment inflicted, the Counsel employed an Arabic word which means to beat severely. The story is commonly notorious amongst the Italian community in Cairo.

I fully recognise, however, in view of Mr. Blunt's denial, that he cannot have been aware of the lengths to which his servants had gone or have himself been present at the beating.

NO. 35.
Mr. W. Blunt to the Marquess of Lansdowne.—(Received September 17.)
My Lord, Fernycroft, Beaulieu, Hants, September 15, 1901.

I HAVE the honour to acknowledge your Lordship's communication of the 11th (received yesterday), with the numerous inclosures. I have gone through these carefully, and, as I conclude that the correspondence on the subject is now complete on your Lordship's part, I will ask to be allowed, on my part, to add a final word.

The thing that strikes me most in reading the notes furnished by Sir Rennell Rodd of the trial and his long pleading in favour of the officers, is the extreme futility and lack of serious importance of the whole original affair. The questions whether the officers did or did not intend to hunt in my garden that Sunday morning, whether Captain Harman did or did not intend his hounds to jump my wall, at what particular moment it was resolved to whip off the hounds, whether they did or did not kill a fox, whether the officers did or did not make themselves understood by my Arab servants, who struck the first blow, who used the foulest language, even who was struck, since nobody was seriously hurt, seems to me of infinitesimal importance compared with the enormous publicity they have received the world over, and the scandal they have occasioned.

I must confess to your Lordship that I am still unconvinced of the superior truth of the amended tale told at the trial at Benha over that told by the officers, and forward to me on the actual day of the occurrence. Also I am too old a sportsman, and too well acquainted with my own property, the direction of its foot-paths, and the habits of its wild animals to accept as less than ludicrous the ingenious but contradictory and quite unsporting excuses made for them by Sir Rennell Rodd. It is not a little significant that the chief personage of the hunt, Captain Harman, master of hounds, the officer who took them up to my garden's edge, who permitted them to leap the wall, who followed them first through my stable yard into my stud farm, with whom the first altercation and collision with my Arab servants took place, of whom Moutlak, usually a shrewd judge of character, is reported to have said that he was "no officer, but worse than a Soudanese syce"—that this gentleman, the head and front of the whole affair, should have been conspicuous at the trial at Benha only by his absence from the witness-box (as the notes of the trial indicate).

I am struck, too, with the extreme meagreness of the evidence offered by the prosecution and with the absence, in the notes, of all evidence on the other side. Hardly less trivial is the way in which Sir Rennell Rodd meets my explanation of the difficulties which lie in the path of justice in the Courts of the provincial Cadis when he cites, in illustration of them, the records of the Cairo police courts, and when he expresses a fear lest my remarks on their less than complete independence of English influences should wound the feelings of the native Judges of Appeal. All these things strike me, in reading the papers through, as astonishingly inadequate. But I recognize that it is not worth while to continue bandying words about them and that, now that my men are all but one out of prison, while the last will be liberated in a week, I may leave the matter where it stands, renewing only my request that your Lordship will publish in its entirety my correspondence with you and Lord Cranborne, including my first letter of the 25th July. Together they present my case sufficiently.

One thing only stands out quite distinctly and seriously in this otherwise not very serious affair, and that is that General Lane and Mr. Machell between them, with the approval of Sir Rennell Rodd, tried to repair the foolish position in which these young officers had placed themselves and their compromised dignity, by endeavouring to get a conviction of a vindictive character against the Arabs (while the circumstances were hushed up in the local press and as far as was possible, through a misleading telegram, in the press at home), taking as the basis of their prosecution Article 220 of the Egyptian Penal Code, an Article never intended, nor, as I am informed, ever before used in cases of common assault, and pressed for the three years' penalty provided in it. Fortunately—and here I admit that I assumed too much in my letter to your Lordship of the 10th August—it was found impossible to prevail even on the Christian Coptic Cadi of the County Court to go as far as this, although to impress him more strongly, the high dignitaries of the Government with the English officers in uniform, and carrying their swords, were present, with places on the bench reserved for them; and all that could be actually obtained was a sentence of six months.

However, the thing is past and finished now, and, as I have said, my men are out of prison. I do not consider that justice has been otherwise than wronged.' But I have been long enough mixed up with public affairs to know that in conflicts between an individual and the full force of a Government, whether in the East or in the West, the balance generally dips on the Government side, and I do not much complain.

All that besides this I will ask of your Lordship is

that, in as much as your Lordship blames me for the order I gave my servants, and as the issue of the trial seems to prove that it is illegal in Egypt to eject by force mounted or armed intruders even from walled lands, your Lordship will consult with Lord Cromer before he returns to Egypt how best my property with its valuable stud and, may I add, the half tame animals in my garden should be protected. I cannot help thinking that it ought to be within Lord Cromer's power and influence to add to his many Egyptian reforms a sufficient law of trespass that should be enforceable against mounted or armed Europeans.

In conclusion I will take this occasion—the last one, I hope, in the present correspondence—to express my regret for having in my published letter made fun, more than was quite their due, of the officers of the 11th Hussars and especially of Major Rycroft, who seems really to have acted on wise and prudent principles in appeasing the trouble, on the 21st July, he had helped to raise. His evidence of his own conduct and motives I accept as quite sincere, while I venture to assure him, through your Lordship, that I never doubted his personally fearless character. But, at the time I wrote my letter to the "Standard" and "Daily News", he should remember that he had my men fast by the heels in prison, that I was without information more than what was given in his own report, which lent itself to raillery, and that raillery seemed my only weapon. I should be sorry if our vendetta should be carried, on either side, farther than it has already gone.

Thanking your Lordship for having allowed me to express myself freely throughout this troublesome affair, I have, &c.

(Signed) WILFRID SCAWEN BLUNT.

NO. 36.

Viscount Cromer to the Marquess of Lansdowne.— (Received September 25.)

12A, Curzon Street, Mayfair, London

My Lord, September 24, 1901.

IN his letter of the 15th instant Mr. Wilfrid Blunt asks that your Lordship should consult with me before I return to Egypt how best his "property, with its valuable stud and the half-tame animals" in his garden, should be protected.

The only suggestion I can make on this point is that Mr. Blunt should repair and possibly raise and enlarge his garden wall. Sir Rennell Rodd, in his letter of the 30th August, points out that, owing to the situation of Mr. Blunt's suburban residence, it enjoys somewhat special facilities for police protection.

As regards Mr. Blunt's suggestion that the general law of trespass in Egypt should be amended, I will, on my return to Cairo, consult the legal advisers of the Egyptian Government on the necessity and also as to the practicability of making any changes. My present impression is that the wisest course will be to leave the matter alone.

I regret to notice that Mr. Blunt, in his letter of the 15th instant, whilst making some sort of apology for the insulting expressions he used towards Major Rycroft, makes use of language only slightly less offensive in speaking of the conduct of Captain Harman, Sir Rennell Rodd, Major-General Lane, and Mr. Machell. The accusations and insinuations made against these gentlemen do not stand in need of refutation.

I have, &c.

(Signed) CROMER

NO. 37.

The Marquess of Lansdowns to Sir R. Rodd.

Sir,   Foreign Office, September 27, 1901

WITH reference to previous correspondence respecting the assault committed on British officers by the servants on Mr. Blunt's property near Cairo, I transmit to you herewith copies of a letter which was addressed to Mr. Blunt by my direction on the subject and of his reply (Nos. 33 and 35). I inclose also a copy of a letter from Lord Cromer, to whom I referred Mr. Blunt's communication (No. 36).

I agree in Lord Cromer's view that Mr. Blunt's observations do not require further notice or reply.

Your proceedings in the matter and your reports upon it have my entire approval.

I am, &c.

(Signed) LANSDOWNE

Other titles in the series

John Profumo and Christine Keeler, 1963

"The story must start with Stephen Ward, aged fifty. The son of a clergymen, by profession he was an osteopath ... his skill was very considerable and he included among his patients many well-known people ...Yet at the same time he was utterly immoral."

The Backdrop
The beginning of the '60s saw the publication of 'Lady Chatterley's Lover' and the dawn of sexual and social liberation as traditional morals began to be questioned and in some instances swept away.

The Book
In spite of the spiralling spate of recent political falls from grace, The Profumo Affair remains the biggest scandal ever to hit British politics. The Minister of War was found to be having an affair with a call girl who had associations with a Russian Naval Officer at the height of the Cold War. There are questions of cover-up, lies told to Parliament, bribery and stories sold to the newspapers. Lord Denning's superbly written report into the scandal describes with astonishment and fascinated revulsion the extraordinary sexual behaviour of the ruling classes. Orgies, naked bathing, sado-masochistic gatherings of the great and good and ministers and judges cavorting in masks are all uncovered.

ISBN 0 11 702402 3

The Loss of the Titanic, 1912

"From 'Mesabe' to 'Titanic'· and all east bound ships. Ice report in Latitude 42N to 41.25N; Longitude 49 to 50.30W. Saw much Heavy Pack Ice and a great number of Large Icebergs. Also Field Ice. Weather good. Clear."

The Backdrop

The watchwords were 'bigger, better, faster, more luxurious' as builders of ocean-going vessels strove to outdo each other as they raced to capitalise on a new golden age of travel.

The Book

The story of the sinking of the Titanic, as told by the official enquiry, reveals some remarkable facts which have been lost in popular re-tellings of the story. A ship of the same line, only a few miles away from the Titanic as she sank, should have been able to rescue passengers, so why did this not happen? Readers of this fascinating report will discover that many such questions remain unanswered and that the full story of a tragedy which has entered into popular mythology has by no means been told.

ISBN 0 11 702403 1

Tragedy at Bethnal Green, 1943

"Immediately the alert was sounded a large number of people left their houses in the utmost haste for shelter. A great many were running. Two cinemas at least in the near vicinity disgorged a large number of people and at least three omnibuses set down their passengers outside the shelter."

The Backdrop

The beleaguered East End of London had born much of the brunt of the Blitz but, in 1943, four years into WW2, it seemed that the worst of the bombing was over.

The Book

The new unfinished tube station at Bethnal Green was one of the largest air raid shelters in London. After a warning siren sounded on March 3, 1943, there was a rush to the shelter. By 8.20pm, a matter of minutes after the alarm had sounded, 174 people lay dead, crushed trying to get into the tube station's booking hall. At the official enquiry, questions were asked about the behaviour of certain officials and whether the accident could have been prevented.

ISBN 0 11 702404 X

The Judgement of Nuremberg, 1946

"Efficient and enduring intimidation can only be achieved either by Capital Punishment or by measures by which the relatives of the criminal and the population do not know the fate of the criminal. This aim is achieved when the criminal is transferred to Germany."

The Backdrop

WW2 is over, there is a climate of jubilation and optimism as the Allies look to rebuilding Europe for the future but the perpetrators of Nazi War Crimes have yet to be reckoned with, and the full extent of their atrocities is as yet widely unknown.

The Book

Today, we have lived with the full knowledge of the extent of Nazi atrocities for over half a century and yet they still retain their power to shock. Imagine what it was like as they were being revealed in the full extent of their horror for the first time. In this book the Judges at the Nuremberg Trials take it in turn to describe the indictments handed down to the defendants and their crimes. The entire history, purpose and method of the Nazi party since its foundation in 1918 is revealed and described in chilling detail.

ISBN 0 11 702406 6

The Boer War: Ladysmith and Mafeking, 1900

"4th February – From General Sir. Redfers Buller to Field-Marshall Lord Roberts … I have today received your letter of 26 January. White keeps a stiff upper lip, but some of those under him are desponding. He calculates he has now 7000 effectives. They are eating their horses and have very little else. He expects to be attacked in force this week … "

The Backdrop

The Boer War is often regarded as one of the first truly modern wars, as the British Army, using traditional tactics, came close to being defeated by a Boer force which deployed what was almost a guerrilla strategy in punishing terrain.

The Book

Within weeks of the outbreak of fighting in South Africa, two sections of the British Army were besieged at Ladysmith and Mafeking. Split into two parts, the book begins with despatches describing the losses at Spion Kop on the way to rescue the garrison at Ladysmith, followed by the army report as the siege was lifted. In the second part is Lord Baden Powell's account of the siege of Mafeking and how the soldiers and civilians coped with the hardship and waited for relief to arrive.

ISBN 0 11 702408 2

The British Invasion Tibet:
Colonel Younghusband, 1904

"On the 13th January I paid ceremonial visit to the Tibetans at Guru, six miles further down the valley in order that by informal discussion might assure myself of their real attitude. There were present at the interview three monks and one general from Lhasa … these monks were low-bred persons, insolent, rude and intensely hostile; the generals, on the other hand, were polite and well-bred."

The Backdrop

At the turn of the century, the British Empire was at its height, with its army in the forefront of the mission to bring what it saw as the tremendous civilising benefits of the British way of life to what it regarded as nations still languishing in the dark ages.

The Book

In 1901, a British Missionary Force under the leadership of Colonel Francis Younghusband crossed over the border from British India and invaded Tibet. Younghusband insisted on the presence of the Dalai Lama at meetings to give tribute to the British and their empire. The Dalai Lama merely replied that he must withdraw. Unable to tolerate such an insolent attitude, Younghusband marched forward and inflicted considerable defeats on the Tibetans in several onesided battles.

ISBN 0 11 702409 0